Renner Learning Resource Center
Elgin Community College
Elgin, IL 60123

VGM Opportunities Series

OPPORTUNITIES IN
FUND-RAISING
CAREERS

Mark Rowh

Foreword by
Joan Suchorski
Vice President
Council for Resource Development

 **VGM Career Books**
NTC/Contemporary Publishing Group

Library of Congress Cataloging-in-Publication Data

Rowh, Mark.
    Opportunities in fund-raising careers / Mark Rowh ; foreword by Joan Suchorski.
        p.   cm. — (VGM opportunities series)
    Includes bibliographical references.
    ISBN 0-658-00055-1 (cloth) — ISBN 0-658-00485-9 (pbk.)
    1. Fund raising—Vocational guidance.   2. Fund raisers (Persons)   3. Nonprofit
organizations.   I. Title.   II. Series.

HV41.2 .R69   2000
361.7'63'0681—dc21

                                                                              00-43637

331.7361
R8810

Cover photograph copyright © Romilly Lockyer/Image Bank

Published by VGM Career Books
A division of NTC/Contemporary Publishing Group, Inc.
4255 West Touhy Avenue, Lincolnwood (Chicago), Illinois 60712-1975 U.S.A.
Copyright © 2001 by NTC/Contemporary Publishing Group, Inc.
Printed in the United States of America
International Standard Book Number: 0-658-00055-1 (cloth)
                                                             0-658-00485-9 (paper)

01   02   03   04   05   06   LB   15   14   13   12   11   10   9   8   7   6   5   4   3   2   1

DEDICATION

This book is dedicated to Jenny Anne.

CONTENTS

The nature of nonprofit organizations. Functions of fund-raising personnel. Sources of funds. Traits needed for a career in fund-raising.

Demand for fund-raising professionals. What fund-raising professionals do. Types of fund-raising positions. Employers of fund-raising professionals. Open to diversity. Flexible career prospects.

Basic development officer jobs. Senior-level development positions. Specialized functions of development officers. Typical job descriptions. Working conditions.

Sources of grant funds. The grant making process. Need for grant writers. Duties performed. Acquiring grant writing skills. Traits needed for success in grant writing.

ABOUT THE AUTHOR

Mark Rowh is an experienced fund-raising professional with more than twenty years of experience in soliciting private funds, writing grant proposals, managing endowed funds, and providing overall leadership for the institutional advancement function in two-year and four-year colleges. He is currently Director of Institutional Advancement at New River Community College in Dublin, Virginia, and he serves as president of the Virginia Organization for Resource Development.

Rowh is also a widely published writer on career topics. He has contributed several other books to various VGM Career Books series and is the author of *Great Jobs for Chemistry Majors, Great Jobs for Political Science Majors, Slam Dunk Cover Letters,* and a number of other books.

He holds a master's degree in English and a doctorate in education.

FOREWORD

Do you have good communication skills? Has anyone ever complimented your ability to organize things? Do you enjoy the thought of doing work that improves the lives of other people? If your answer to these questions is "yes," you might be a candidate for a career in fund-raising.

Raising money and other support for nonprofit organizations is the main function for this challenging career area. Thousands of organizations throughout the United States and Canada rely in whole or in part on private donations for support of their activities. Everyone knows about groups such as the Red Cross, the American Cancer Society, and Habitat for Humanity. But for every big-name organization, there are many others that also depend on private donations to fulfill their missions. In your local area, chances are an array of schools, colleges, hospitals, social action groups, and other organizations also rely on voluntary contributions to serve their publics.

The key word here is "voluntary." People do not have to give money to nonprofit organizations. They can choose to make donations or not to make them. They can give large amounts or small. They might decide to support one but reject others. They may give to an organization one time but never make a repeat gift, or they may become regular contributors over a period of years.

The diversity of these options is the main reason for the emergence of an important career area—that of the fund-raising professional. With so many choices before them, donors need information, assistance, and encouragement in directing their support toward appropriate purposes. At the same time, nonprofit organizations need people who will perform this important function. Thus a continuing demand exists for workers who are knowledgeable and skilled in this process.

Are you interested in becoming one of these professionals? If so, the material provided in this book will be of interest. You will learn about the types of jobs available, the duties involved, the skills required, and the challenges that come with a fund-raising career. Read on, and perhaps you will find that this career path holds possibilities for you.

Joan Suchorski
Vice President
Council for Resource Development

ACKNOWLEDGMENTS

The author offers grateful thanks to the following for their cooperation in providing information for this book:

American Cancer Society
Association for Healthcare Philanthropy
Canadian Centre for Philanthropy
Case Western Reserve University
City University of New York
Council for Advancement and Support of Education
Council on Foundations
Council for Resource Development
Diana Hardison
Indiana University
National Society of Fund-Raising Executives
Seton Hall University
Society for Nonprofit Organizations
University of Virginia
U.S. Department of Labor
U.S. General Services Administration
Virginia Organization for Resource Development

INTRODUCTION

The charitable contribution is a time-honored tradition. Individuals, corporations, and others donate money or other resources to nonprofit organizations. The purposes are nearly as diverse as the people who make these contributions: scholarships to help deserving students attend college, projects to save endangered animal species, research to cure troublesome diseases, and more.

Such donations have become so important to many nonprofit organizations that they depend on them to fulfill their missions. For some groups, their budgets come entirely from donations or grant funds. For others, contributed funds are not the only source of financial support, but they are, nevertheless, an important one.

Given the importance of external support, many organizations employ professionals to raise the funds they need. The men and women in these roles enjoy truly challenging careers. Their work is important in making sure that the organizations fulfill their goals. This is not just a matter of dollars and cents but of meeting genuine societal needs. Fund-raising professionals can take great satisfaction in doing work that improves the world or at least a small piece of it.

How would you feel about coordinating a fund-raising campaign that results in a new wing being built for a children's hospital? Or garnering a donation that allows a talented student to go to college? Or helping an elderly couple plan a donation that will support the arts in your community? These are just a few examples of the key roles played by fund-raising professionals.

A career in fund-raising takes hard work and dedication. But it also offers great rewards. For those with the right interests and abilities, a career in this area can be a great way to combine personal interests with a commitment to something larger than oneself.

In short, fund-raising isn't just about money. It's also about making good things happen that improve society. The thousands of people who work in this area contribute enormously through their knowledge, talent, and commitment to the needs of various organizations. As such needs grow and as existing personnel retire, there will be a demand for new people to take on these challenges. Perhaps you could be one of them.

Opportunities in Fund-Raising Careers presents an overview of the fund-raising field in general and the specific nature of several types of positions. If a career in this area sounds appealing, you are invited to read further and check things out. In the process, keep in mind that thanks to the work of dedicated professionals throughout the United States and Canada, this is a career field with increasing impact and growing stature.

CHAPTER 1

FUNDING FOR NONPROFIT ENTERPRISES

Fund-raising professionals perform some of the most important work in our society. They are the people who help nonprofit organizations obtain the money and other support needed to carry out their activities.

THE NATURE OF NONPROFIT ORGANIZATIONS

Nonprofit organizations hold a special place in modern society. Unlike corporations, small businesses, or other similar concerns, it is not their mission to earn a profit. Instead, the overall goal of nonprofits is to meet some societal need, be it for the public at large or for a very narrow group with specific needs.

For example, the American Lung Society is an organization devoted to promoting good health, with an obvious focus on human respiratory systems as the name makes clear. As a nonprofit organization, its goals and methods of operating are different from, say, a company that manufacturers special breathing equipment for asthma sufferers. While both fulfill important functions, the equipment company's most basic goal is making money. It sells equipment for more than the cost of manufacturing it, with profits going to those who own the company. If it is unable to make a profit, the company eventually will cease to exist.

The American Lung Society, on the other hand, exists for a different purpose. It supports research in combating lung disease, conducts no-smoking campaigns, and produces educational materials about lung health, among other functions. It does not attempt to make a profit, but that does not mean there is no need for funds. To the contrary, all of these activities require substantial funding for everything from paying the salaries of employees to printing and mailing promotional materials. Since the organization does not obtain the bulk of its revenues by selling products or services, it must look elsewhere for funding—voluntary donations.

The same is true for other nonprofit organizations. In some cases, donations make up most or all of the funding base. In other instances, they supplement other sources. For example, most private colleges rely on tuition and fees paid by students and their families, investment income generated by previously donated funds, government grants and student aid, and some other sources of support. But added together, all of these funds still may not be enough to provide all the programs and services needed by students or sponsored by the college in support of its mission. So as an extra source of income, colleges solicit donations from alumni, corporations, and others who believe in the institution and its goals.

Similarly, state-supported colleges and universities also count on private funding to support scholarships, professional development for faculty and staff, athletic programs, and a variety of "extras" not covered by students' tuition or government allocations.

A similar story holds true at differing levels and in different funding combinations at hospitals, research agencies, social welfare groups, and other nonprofit organizations. Without substantial funding in the form of donations from other organizations or individuals, one of two things would happen: The organization would find it necessary to reduce the breadth or level of services provided, or it would completely stop operating.

Given the importance of external funding, it is not surprising that a specialized group of positions has emerged in recent decades. While to some degree general management staff may be responsible for raising funds along with other duties, many organizations employ specialists in this area. In a very small organization, this may consist of one position, which may be part-time or full-time. In a larger one, scores of staff may be assigned to this function. In either case, the people who hold these jobs play an important role in making the organization successful.

FUNCTIONS OF FUND-RAISING PERSONNEL

The person who specializes in fund-raising devotes his or her energies to bringing in external support for an organization. The actual duties may vary widely, depending on the organization's mission and size and the degree to which the position is specialized. In general, such duties include some combination of the following:

- designing programs and activities to encourage contributions or other external support
- soliciting donations from individuals, foundations, corporations, or others
- maintaining positive relationships with donors or potential donors
- managing fund-raising activities or related efforts such as the investment of donated funds
- writing proposals for grants or donations
- conducting research on prospective donors or maintaining background information about donors or prospective contributors

- coordinating special events
- conducting, coordinating, or supervising related activities such as public relations or marketing efforts

Fund-raising is big business! By the end of 1999, Duke University and Cornell University each had raised more than $1 billion in recent campaigns, and Harvard and Columbia had passed the $2 billion mark. We're talking *billions* here, not millions! Organizations such as the American Cancer Society, the March of Dimes, and many others are also very large players on the fund-raising scene, not to mention churches and other religious organizations.

At the other end of the spectrum are small groups serving less ambitious needs. For purposes such as a local teen center or a program for abused spouses, annual fund-raising totals may be much less dramatic. But they are important nonetheless.

Consider these facts reported by the American Association of Fund-Raising Counsel:

- In 1998, Americans contributed more than $174 billion to nonprofit organizations.
- Giving by individuals topped $134 billion during the same period.
- Noncorporate foundations donated more than $17 billion.
- Corporations contributed nearly $9 billion.
- Giving from bequests exceeded $13 billion.

In any given year, the largest share of donated funds goes to religious denominations and congregations. Other popular targets of the generosity of donors include health, human services, environmental, and public benefit organizations.

Regardless of the size of the organization or the source of funds, someone must take a leadership role in raising money. Sometimes this is handled by volunteers, but in most organizations where an effective program is in place, it is coordinated by a fund-raising professional.

In the educational sector, fund-raising activities are part of a broad-based area known as development or institutional advancement. The Council for the Advancement and Support of Education (CASE) defines institutional advancement as "a broad field that strengthens education by enhancing its image, keeping alumni involved, raising money, recruiting students, and encouraging close relationships with local, state, and federal governments." Specific areas of institutional advancement include:

- alumni relations
- communications (including publications, publicity, internal communications, community relations, and marketing)
- government relations
- educational fund-raising (including annual giving, capital campaigns, major gifts, planned giving, and grant development)

Outside of education the terms may differ somewhat, but the same types of functions are covered. A frequently used term is "development," meaning basically the same thing as advancement. In any case, the area of fund-raising typically includes not just raising money, but related areas involving creating or sustaining external support for an organization.

SOURCES OF FUNDS

Just where do fund-raising personnel look to obtain support for their organizations?

Probably the most important source of funds for most organizations is the individual citizen who chooses to support that group. Major charities such as the American Heart Association, the Red

Cross, and thousands of others depend heavily on individual men and women to contribute money to support their programs.

Private corporations are another source of significant funding. If you watch public television, attend the Special Olympics, or enjoy programs offered by a museum or planetarium, just to cite a few examples, chances are that private corporations have donated funds in support of these organizations.

Some of the most important sources of funds for nonprofit organizations are foundations. These are nonprofit organizations that, in most cases, hold and invest funds and then use this money as a pool from which they award grants or donations. Types of foundations, according to the nonprofit Council on Foundations, include:

- community foundations
- corporate foundations/giving programs
- family foundations
- private operating foundations
- private independent foundations
- public foundations

Some of the largest American foundations include the Lilly Endowment, the Ford Foundation, the Robert Wood Johnson Foundation, the W. K. Kellogg Foundation, the Andrew W. Mellon Foundation, the Annenberg Foundation, and the Charles Stewart Mott Foundation. Thousands of others also exist, including many smaller foundations serving local communities or addressing a very narrow range of interest areas.

Representative Canadian foundations include the AIDS Foundation of Canada, the Canadian Airlines Foundation, Canadian Pacific Charitable Foundation, Canadian Women's Foundation, Canadian Youth Business Foundation, Cornerstone 52 Foundation, the EJLB Foundation, the EverGreen Foundation, the Walter and Duncan Gordon Foundation, the Heart and Stroke Foundation of Canada, the J. W. McConnell Family Foundation, and the National Aboriginal Achievement Foundation.

According to the Council on Foundations, more than forty-six thousand foundations now exist. This is twice the number of those in existence in 1980. Many of them award grants to nonprofit organizations.

Still another source of funds is the government. In the United States and Canada, government agencies routinely make grant awards to nonprofit organizations. Many of these are awarded on a competitive basis, where applications for funding are submitted and those receiving the best ratings are awarded grant funds. Schools, colleges, social action groups, and many other nonprofit organizations often tap into this funding source.

The number of organizations seeking support from these foundations and others is quite large, with new groups frequently being formed and existing ones often expanding. Competition for funds can be stiff. As a result, the demand for professionals who can bring in such funds continues across all types of organizations.

TRAITS NEEDED FOR A CAREER IN FUND-RAISING

According to Ohio State University, the most important skills needed by those working in nonprofit organizations are people skills, sales skills, and communication skills. Also important are creativity, initiative, presentation skills, and leadership abilities.

Indeed, fund-raising is a diverse area, and people with different combinations of skills can be successful. Generally speaking, though, most of the following skills or traits are needed to perform this kind of work successfully:

1. excellent skills in oral communications
2. the ability to write with clarity, accuracy, and persuasiveness

3. a genuine liking for people and an ability to interact effectively with others (in other words, good "people skills")
4. a high energy level
5. a sense of loyalty and commitment to the employing organization and its purposes
6. a strong sense of personal ethics
7. the ability to solve problems and work creatively to improve processes and procedures
8. good analytical skills
9. an appreciation for the importance of teamwork
10. a value system that does not focus on self-importance but instead emphasizes broad-based goals and shared accomplishments

Questions to Ask Yourself

When you think about it, the term "nonprofit" may be a misleading one. The fact that organizations exist for purposes other than business or commerce may make them seem less substantial than large corporations that employ great numbers of people. Yet the nonprofit sector is actually immense, made up of thousands of organizations. It is a substantial employer but, more importantly, a fundamental part of modern society. Thus it can be an excellent sector in which to pursue a career.

On a personal basis, the appropriateness of a fund-raising career depends not just on the often noble purposes involved, but also on individual talents and interests. In examining whether this might be an area of potential interest to you, ask yourself these questions:

- Do I enjoy working with people?
- Do I have good communication skills?
- Would I be comfortable asking individuals or organizations to make contributions?

- Do others consider me a hard worker?
- Can I work well without a great deal of direct supervision?
- Am I a good team player?
- Would I be comfortable working in a nonprofit organization?
- Am I willing to obtain the necessary academic preparation to prepare for a job in this field?
- Would I be willing to undergo additional training to develop specialized skills to support fund-raising functions?
- Am I good at keeping records and following through on detail work?
- Do I have an orientation toward public community service?

If your answer to most or all of these questions is "yes," you may be well suited to a career in fund-raising. If you're not sure about a number of them, consider ways in which you can evaluate your potential in this area (see Chapter 10 for more tips). The material covered throughout the rest of this book will also help you assess your suitability for this field:

- Chapter 2 covers the role of the fund-raising professional.
- Chapter 3 looks at the development officer's position.
- Chapter 4 covers the work of grant writers.
- Chapter 5 reviews the role of the planned giving specialist.
- Chapter 6 covers fund-raising support jobs.
- Chapter 7 provides an overview of the necessary educational preparation.
- Chapter 8 looks at professional associations and resources.
- Chapter 9 discusses salaries and benefits.
- Chapter 10 provides tips for getting started.

After you've considered the material presented, perhaps you will want to take further steps in pursuing a career in fund-raising. It can definitely be an exciting career area!

CHAPTER 2

THE FUND-RAISING PROFESSIONAL

Raising funds is a specialized process. It requires a combination of skills and knowledge that not everyone possesses. It also takes a major commitment of time. Yet when the proper time is committed by people who are adept at this process, fund-raising can pay off handsomely. Boards that run nonprofit organizations and senior managers realize this; as a result, they have created positions for fund-raising professionals to pursue vital support for their organizations.

DEMAND FOR FUND-RAISING PROFESSIONALS

As noted in the previous chapter, people give away literally billions of dollars. Nonprofit organizations benefit from such donations and, in many cases, depend entirely on them for their existence. Accordingly, the men and women who devote themselves to the fund-raising process play an extremely important role in the nonprofit world. And a great demand exists for their services.

In a single recent issue of the *Chronicle of Philanthropy,* a publication covering the nonprofit sector in the United States and Canada, scores of ads were published for job openings including the following:

- a Regional Development Director at the University of California, Berkeley
- an Events Coordinator at Cold Spring Harbor Laboratory, a biological science research facility in New York
- an Assistant Director of Special Gifts at the University of Delaware
- a Development Coordinator at Covenant House, a New York organization serving homeless and at-risk youth
- an International Advancement Manager in the Office of Development at the University of Washington
- a Development Director at the Texas Archaeological Society
- a Development Manager at the Georgia Conservancy
- a Development Director for the Corporation for Supportive Housing in New York City, an organization focusing on the needs of homeless and disabled people
- an Associate Director, Planned Gifts, and a Specialist, Major Gifts, for the Alzheimer's Association, a national organization with offices in Chicago
- a Director and an Assistant Director of Development for the Albert Einstein College of Medicine in the Bronx, New York
- a Director of Development for the Santa Barbara (California) Museum of Natural History
- an Annual Fund Manager for the National Outdoor Leadership School in Lander, Wyoming
- a Capital Campaign Manager for the Chrysler Museum of Art in Norfolk, Virginia
- a Development Assistant for the Hospital for Special Surgery in New York City
- a Grant Writer/Fund-Raiser for the Natural Resource Defense Council, a national environmental group with headquarters in New York City
- a Planned Giving Officer for the Earthjustice Legal Defense Fund, a nonprofit law firm in San Francisco

- a Director of Major Gifts and Planned Giving for the International Fund for Animal Welfare in Yarmouthport, Massachusetts
- a Director of Planned Giving for the American Cancer Society's Florida division
- a Director of Resource Development for the Council for Advancement and Support of Education (CASE) in Washington, D.C.

At any given time, similar positions are open at organizations around North America. The fund-raising field is certainly not a static one, and opportunities abound for talented workers.

As the previous list also illustrates, fund-raising jobs can be found in a variety of organizations. The people who fulfill these roles play a key role in making those organizations successful. When such positions are considered as a whole, they constitute a broad-based professional field that can be a challenging career area.

WHAT FUND-RAISING PROFESSIONALS DO

Probably the worst stereotype of a fund-raiser is the cartoon character who holds out a tin cup, begging for a handout from passersby. This, or course, is not true.

Instead, those who work in this field are representatives of well-respected organizations. They are professionals who need a substantial level of knowledge of at least two different types. First is a deep understanding of the organizations they represent. A development officer at a college, for example, must know a great deal about education to be an effective representative of the school. Prospective donors may be alumni or others with special interest in the institution. They may want to know about new academic programs or plans for campus facilities. They may voice opinions about the need for educational reform or ask questions about research products being sponsored by the college. To represent the college, the development professional must be well informed and conversant with educational goals and the efforts to meet them.

The same is true in other organizations. A fund-raiser working for the American Cancer Society, for example, should be knowledgeable not only about the organization itself, but also about trends in efforts to control, cure, or prevent cancer.

In addition to this type of knowledge, a second requirement is an understanding of practices related to receiving and managing monetary gifts or other donated resources. The fund-raising professional must have a firm grasp of the practicalities involved in such transactions. Will a gift be tax-deductible? Can a donor specify who will be the recipient of a scholarship? What kind of records must be maintained about a gift of stock or other appreciated securities rather than cash? These are just a few examples of the types of questions a development officer or other professional must be prepared to answer.

It is also important to note that fund-raisers seldom spend their time talking people into donating money that they would otherwise use for other purposes. The truth is that most donors *want* to give. Many times, donors initiate the giving process without even having been asked for donation. Even when "asking" is involved, it is a far cry from begging when done properly. Rather, effective professionals in this area present information to donors, make a case for their organization's needs, and assist people in making decisions about when and how to give. But they do not pry money away from people who do not want to part with it.

In a recent study, the National Society of Fund Raising Executives (NSFRE) found that fund-raisers do not spend a majority of their time asking people for money. In a survey of the organization's members, more than two-thirds of respondents said they spend 20 percent of their time, or less, asking for gifts. Instead, they indicated that most of their time is spent on the following duties:

- managing staff
- coordinating volunteers
- organizing events
- building relationships with potential donors and the public

In fact, building relationships with donors was the responsibility most frequently cited as requiring the most time.

The same survey found that fund-raisers are adapting to the new challenges of the fund-raising profession such as use of electronic technologies. More than 80 percent of respondents said they use e-mail regularly, and over half use the Internet at least once a day.

On a daily basis, fund-raisers do much of the work common to managers in many settings. In a given day, a fund-raising professional may perform some or all of the following tasks:

- hold meetings with potential donors, staff, or others
- talk on the phone with donors, colleagues within the same organization, or others
- use a computer to communicate via e-mail, seek out information on the Internet, or obtain data
- write thank you letters, memos, or reports
- write proposals to request funds or seek support for organizational initiatives
- plan or attend a social function such as a reception or dedication ceremony
- give a speech
- hire a new staff member
- conduct a performance evaluation for an existing staff member
- develop publicity plans

Depending on the level of responsibility, a fund-raising job may be considered a management position or a support staff role. But regardless of the level within an organization, this job consists of demanding work worthy of respect from others both inside the field and beyond.

TYPES OF FUND-RAISING POSITIONS

Titles of fund-raising positions vary. The titles often are quite similar but with differences based on organizational preferences. In many cases, they provide a good indicator of the degree to which duties for a given position are specialized.

Here are some representative job titles:

Annual Fund Coordinator
Annual Giving Manager
Assistant Director of Development
Assistant Vice President for Federal Relations
Associate Director of Capital Projects
Associate Director of Development
Chief Development Officer
Development Associate
Development Coordinator
Development Officer
Director of Advancement
Director of Annual Fund
Director of Corporate and Foundation Relations
Director of Corporate Relations
Director of Development
Director of Development and Communications
Director of Institutional Advancement
Director of Major and Planned Gifts
Director of Planning and Grants
Executive Director of the Foundation
Executive Director of Major Gifts
Fund-Raising Assistant
Fund-Raising Director
Grant Writer
Grants Director
Grants Manager

Major Gifts Officer
Major Gifts Representative
Manager of Corporate Giving
National Campaign Director
Planned Giving Officer
Program Officer
Senior Development Officer
Senior Planned Giving Officer
Senior Program Officer
Vice President for Advancement
Vice President for Development
Vice President for Institutional Advancement
Vice President for Resource Development

As titles indicate (at least in part), some jobs in fund-raising fit into the category of upper management. Others may be considered more in terms of middle management, and some represent entry-level positions. The variety of jobs bodes well for those interested in pursuing fund-raising careers. Not only is there a broad range of job possibilities for less experienced personnel, but good potential also exists for advancing on the job as additional experience is gained.

EMPLOYERS OF FUND-RAISING PROFESSIONALS

The sample jobs mentioned previously give an idea of the types of employers who support positions in fund-raising. Most employers are nonprofit organizations, although private consulting firms and other businesses can also be employers of workers whose jobs are related to the fund-raising process.

Some major employers of fund-raising professionals include:

national charities
regional and local charities

four-year colleges and universities
community colleges
private elementary and secondary schools
hospitals
research organizations
environmental action groups
political campaigns
human rights organizations
museums
zoos
religious organizations
educational associations
performing arts organizations

These are just some examples of the many types of organizations relying on professional employees to foster external support for their purposes and needs. With such variety, it is obvious that fund-raising is by no means a narrowly defined career area.

OPEN TO DIVERSITY

A strength of fund-raising as a career area is that it is a truly diverse one. People from all kinds of backgrounds can find a place in this field.

While there may be no such thing as a typical fund-raising professional, the NSFRE survey cited earlier in this chapter found that a representative member of that national fund-raising organization would be a Caucasion female between thirty-five and fifty-five years of age who holds at least a baccalaureate degree and works for a not-for-profit organization involved in education, health services, or social services.

At the same time, many minority professionals work in fund-raising, as do people from different age groups and those representing a wide range of issues.

In fact, fund-raising is one area where people can take major steps to support their convictions. Are you passionate about saving rain forests? Protecting endangered species? Prohibiting abortions? Supporting the pro-choice movement? Helping children have better lives? Whatever your interest, chances are that nonprofit organizations exist to advocate your beliefs. And professional fund-raisers can help them achieve their goals.

FLEXIBLE CAREER PROSPECTS

A major advantage of a career in fund-raising is that it can offer flexible prospects. With the right training and experience, a skilled worker in this area can enjoy excellent prospects for moving up to higher level positions or for moving into related career areas.

Since many of the skills involved are transferable to other job areas, the potential exists to move into other careers if that is desired. For example, skilled fund-raisers may easily move into sales positions in the private sector. Those who have held significant management responsibilities may find they can use those skills to perform other management jobs in nonprofit organizations. As just one example, the chief development officer in a college or university setting may eventually vie for the position of president of the institution. In a large charity, it would not be unusual to find that the executive director had originally held a fund-raising position.

Or, in another case, a development officer might leave a nonprofit organization and take a job with a private consulting firm. In this position, the former fund-raiser advises organizations on fund-raising strategies, conducts feasibility studies, and helps conduct fund-raising campaigns. A different career path for the same individual might entail developing software, selling it to nonprofit organizations, and training staff to use it.

Even if an entire career is spent working for nonprofits, there are thousands of organizations across North America that need the services of talented fund-raising professionals. Such flexibility can be a real asset in an era when job mobility may be an important factor in selecting or following a given career path. The diversity of career prospects to be found in fund-raising and related areas means that for any individual, a broad range of opportunities might be pursued.

CHAPTER 3

DEVELOPMENT OFFICER

Probably the most basic, single fund-raising position is that of the development officer or development director. In a small organization, if only one fund-raising position exists, this will probably be it. In a larger organization, a number of development officers may work concurrently to carry out the overall fund-raising program.

BASIC DEVELOPMENT OFFICER JOBS

A person just getting started in fund-raising may hold any of several jobs. Many entry-level positions grow into other jobs with similar responsibilities, but with more autonomy. For example, a recent college graduate may start out as a development associate or assistant and then progress to a coordinator's position.

Such a position may be the only one within an organization, or it may be one of many. At a large university, for example, scores of workers may hold similar positions but handle different specific assignments. Some may raise funds for the college of engineering, others for the college of business, and others for different departments. Responsibilities for such a position generally include some combination of the following:

- supporting an identified segment of a major fund-raising program or a combination of development projects in support of the overall university development program

- developing, planning, scheduling, initiating, and coordinating a combination of fund-raising programs and projects
- conducting research about possible funding sources
- soliciting funds from sources such as foundations, corporations, and individuals
- writing grant proposals
- coordinating the work of volunteers
- coordinating arrangements for special events
- writing correspondence and designing publications
- developing and managing project budgets
- writing summary reports or other types of reports
- supervising support staff, interns, and student workers
- performing related tasks

The background and experience needed for such positions varies. Generally, one would require at least a bachelor's degree in a field such as public relations, English, marketing, communications, or another liberal arts area. Those with previous experience in activities related to fund-raising naturally will have an inside track over other applicants.

In smaller organizations, development officers may have similar duties but will be part of a less extensive staff. Their duties will be similar in nature, but they will represent the entire organization rather than just a single organizational unit. Or, they may be assigned to specific types of fund-raising activities.

SENIOR-LEVEL DEVELOPMENT POSITIONS

The highest-level fund-raising position in a nonprofit organization is usually that of director, executive director, or vice president. Generally, this position differs from other fund-raising jobs in that it includes substantial management responsibilities.

In many organizations, particularly colleges, the top-ranking fund-raising professional is also referred to as the chief development officer. This somewhat general term brings a level of consistency to a position that can be called by many other names. For example, those holding the jobs of vice president for advancement, director of institutional advancement, or executive director of development could all hold the chief development officer's position at their respective organizations.

As previously noted, the use of titles varies widely. In part, the size of the organization determines use of appropriate job titles. For example, in a large organization, a director of development may report to a vice president, who is the chief development officer. In a smaller organization, the director of development may be the chief development officer or even the only development professional.

Regardless of titles, most senior development officers tend to have responsibilities such as the following:

- working closely with the president or chief executive officer of the employing organization
- working directly with board members and prominent supporters of the organization
- planning, implementing, and evaluating fund-raising activities
- supervising the organization's entire advancement operation
- hiring, supervising, and evaluating staff members
- representing the organization to a variety of publics

SPECIALIZED FUNCTIONS
OF DEVELOPMENT OFFICERS

While some development officers carry out a broad range of responsibilities, others focus on specific types of giving or on a narrow range of duties. Here are some representative specialty areas:

Annual giving. Development officers who focus on annual giving encourage donors to become regular, yearly contributors to the organization. Their duties range from identifying potential donors in the first place, to encouraging repeat donors to increase their level of giving as time passes.

Alumni affairs. Alumni affairs personnel can be found at most colleges and universities. Among other duties, they keep former students informed about the institution, focusing both on the school's accomplishments and its continuing need for monetary support.

Capital campaigns. Capital giving refers to making large gifts during specific campaigns as opposed to routine annual giving. At one time tending to focus on the need for new buildings, capital campaigns now cover a wide range of needs such as scholarship support, endowed chairs for faculty, research support, and other needs. Some development officers are employed specifically to work on one portion of a capital campaign.

Major gifts. Every gift is important, but very large gifts are treasured because they can make a major impact on an organization. In some instances, development officers are assigned specifically to seek out larger gifts. For example, one position might focus only on gifts or potential donations of at least $10,000 or, perhaps, of $100,000. In some cases, the preferred amount is even larger; there are a few development officers who deal only with donations of $1 million or more. Frequently, seeking major gifts is a responsibility included among other duties, with no specific guidelines on the size of gifts.

Communications. In a narrow context, communications in the advancement area may refer to the development of brochures, campaign literature, annual reports, and other publications that support fund-raising. In a broader sense, the area of communications includes conveying information about the entire organization to the public. This can include functions such a public information, public relations, advertising, marketing, and development of publications.

Individuals who work within this area are often considered a part of the advancement team, and the chief development officer frequently supervises such functions.

Government relations. Relationships with government agencies have a direct bearing on fund-raising, whether that means influencing legislation or pursuing funding through government grants and contracts. Development officers may include government relations as part of their responsibilities and, in some cases, may have this as their primary function.

Proposal development. While individuals often make donations based on personal conversations, letters of request, telephone solicitations, or simply the demand to give, a different process is usually involved with funding from organizations. For foundations, government agencies, and other organizations, a common mechanism is the submission of written proposals for funding. Development officers frequently write proposals as a part of their duties, and proposal development is an important function within the overall fund-raising area. As discussed in more detail in Chapter 4, some positions focus entirely on the grant-writing process.

Planned giving. Many donations to nonprofit organizations come in the form of planned gifts. Such donations usually involve contractual arrangements in which gifts may be made over a period of time, ownership of securities or land is transferred but the donors still receive income, or through some other type of arrangement. Many development officers perform functions related to planned giving, and some focus on planned giving as their primary function (see Chapter 5).

Foundation management. Some public organizations are affiliated with private foundations that exist solely to support the needs of the sponsoring organization. For example, many state-supported colleges and universities have established foundations that serve as tools for raising money, investing funds, or otherwise providing support. Quite often, development officers are actually employed by these foundations, even though they are really seeking support for the college in question. Or they may be employed by the college, but spend a portion of their time managing foundation affairs. In either case, working with an affiliated foundation is a common duty of development officers working for some types of publicly funded foundations.

These are just some functions performed by development officers. Others include conducting prospect research or other research related to fund-raising, coordinating special events, managing investments generated by the fund-raising process, conducting short- and long-range planning, supporting economic development initiatives, managing volunteers and staff members, and, in some cases, completing tasks that are not directly related to fund-raising, but that support the overall goals of the organization (for example, serving on a planning committee).

TYPICAL JOB DESCRIPTIONS

A look at actual position descriptions for development officer positions can be revealing. Following is a typical job announcement for a recent opening as a Manager of Corporate and Foundation Gifts for the Seattle Public Library:

Responsibilities: Researching, developing, and securing gifts and grants from corporations and foundations.

Reporting: Works under the supervision of the Director of Development/Director of the Capital Campaign.

Duties:

— Plan, organize, manage, and monitor the raising of major gifts from corporations and foundations as part of the Library Foundation's capital campaign.
— Research corporate and foundation prospects.
— Develop cultivation and solicitation strategies.
— Maintain current and accurate prospect files.
— Write and produce solicitation materials for each prospect, developing special campaign materials as needed.
— Support, train, motivate, and manage volunteers who will assist with the solicitations.
— Serve as staff support to the Corporate and Foundation Gifts Task Group.
— Track the progress of the task group and ensure that meetings are set, agendas developed, notices sent, minutes distributed, and assignments carried out.
— Create partnerships and secure support to help underwrite special projects, programs, and equipment needs beyond the period of the capital campaign.
— Ensure the timely and appropriate acknowledgment of all gifts within area of responsibility.
— Assist in the development of donor recognition/appreciation strategies.
— Become familiar with the culture and values of the library and approach all tasks and responsibilities with those in mind.

Qualifications:

— Baccalaureate degree in Liberal Arts, Communications, Marketing, or a related field.
— A minimum of five years of successful experience in raising corporate and foundation gifts.
— Strong leadership qualities.
— Excellent skills in both verbal and written communications.
— Good word processing skills.

— Imagination, flexibility, good organization, and project management skills.
— Ability to use initiative and independent judgment in a wide variety of situations.
— Outstanding people and volunteer management skills, including the ability to work with people of different backgrounds, personalities, and working styles.
— Ability to develop and maintain effective working relationships with staff, campaign leadership, the Foundation Board, and other community organizations.
— Ability to represent the Library and its Foundation effectively in a variety of settings and with diverse groups.
— Ability to occasionally work a varied schedule as meetings dictate.

If this description sounds imposing, just keep in mind that it represents an example of a well-organized, established fundraising effort. Many smaller organizations offer entry-level positions with much less experience required. Here is a brief description for the job of Director of Development of the National Senior Citizens Law Center in Washington, DC, an organization providing advocacy and support for disadvantaged older Americans.

Reporting: The Development Director reports to the Executive Director and works closely with Board members and staff.

Responsibilities:

— Direct, hands-on solicitation of major gifts from family foundations, individuals, and firms.
— Development of a broad-based, general contributions program.
— Creation of a planned giving program.
— Maintenance of a development database.
— Oversight of an aggressive public relations effort.

Qualifications:

— Successful experience in fund-raising with a record in solicitation of major gifts.
— Knowledge of family foundations.
— Enthusiasm for a challenge.
— Computer competence.
— A strong commitment to program work.

Here is another example of a position in a smaller organization, the Texas Archeological Society:

Position: Director of Development

Responsibilities:

— Carry out fund-raising to support existing Society programs and develop new initiatives as outlined in the organization's strategic plan.
— Initiate fund-raising campaigns targeting individuals, foundations, and corporations to raise funds for public education, media outreach (a popular magazine and video news releases), publication enhancement, and organizational development.
— Carry out individual fund-raising within a 1,200-member statewide society.
— Develop a plan for tracking donations and reporting to granting agencies.
— Promote new initiatives to increase Society membership and enhance public visibility.
— Attend quarterly meetings and participate in Society activities.
— Serve as spokesperson to public, private, and governmental agencies.

Qualifications:

— Self-motivation and ability to work well independently while communicating with the Society's leadership.
— A minimum of five years' experience in nonprofit management and fund development.

— Interest in historic preservation and in archaeological issues.
— Business and/or management background.
— Strong communication and computer skills.
— Minimum of a bachelor's degree.

Here is a brief description for the position of Vice President for Institutional Advancement at a public university:

Reporting: Reports directly to the President; works closely with Deans, other University officers, the Directors of the University's Education Foundation, the Alumni Association, and various advisory boards.

Duties: Plans and directs the university's fund-raising programs. Areas of responsibility include the following:

— Major gifts
— Annual funding
— Planned giving
— Corporate giving
— Foundation giving
— Alumni program

Qualifications:

— Bachelor's degree required; advanced degree preferred.
— Five years of progressively responsible development experience, or similarly transferable work experience, preferably in a college or university environment.
— Familiarity with charitable giving techniques and demonstrated ability to work effectively with a variety of constituencies.
— Excellent motivational skills.
— Experience in a leadership role in a major fund-raising campaign preferred.

As another example, following is a description for the Executive Director of the Foundation at the Florida Community College at Jacksonville, a large two-year college:

Duties:

— Provide collegewide leadership and direction in the for-
  mulation, recommendation, implementation, control, and
  evaluation of rules, policies, procedures, guidelines, and
  plans related to private sector resource development.
— Recommend organizational structure, personnel staffing
  patterns, and job responsibilities for effective performance within the college for the purpose of generating
  donated income.
— Develop and implement comprehensive private sector resource development initiatives to broaden the community's awareness of the College and increase private
  contributions to the College (initiatives may include, but
  are not limited to, annual giving, major gifts, alumni and
  planned giving programs).
— Cooperate with other college staff to support institutional
  advancement.
— Represent the College as a spokesperson to external constituencies for the development and advancement of the
  College.

Qualifications:

— Bachelor's degree and successful fund-raising experience
  (graduate degree with higher education development experience preferred).

WORKING CONDITIONS

Regardless of the position involved, most people who work in
fund-raising or related fields enjoy comfortable working environments. Development officers tend to do most of their work in offices as well as conference rooms and other similar surroundings.

Generally, development directors and other officers spend a significant amount of time in their own private offices. Such settings may vary in size and overall appearance, from a small, simple cubicle or room to a large, well-appointed office. In some cases, this is directly related to factors such as level of authority and seniority. Obviously, a vice president in a college or other nonprofit organization is more likely to enjoy a large or impressive office than would lower-ranking staff. But seniority or rank is not the only factor involved. Other considerations may include the size and age of the building in which an office is located, the overall size and funding level of the employing organization, and other factors.

Whether it is large or small, simple or plush, a typical office will include basics such as a desk, chair, telephone, and computer. Larger offices may include conference tables, side chairs, and other furniture. In addition to work completed within their own offices, development officers may spend time in related work environments such as conference rooms, offices of co-workers, homes of potential donors, restaurants where business luncheons or dinners are held, hotel conference rooms, and other locations.

Many fund-raising positions require substantial amounts of travel. This may include traveling to meet with donors or potential donors at their businesses or homes, attending professional conferences, and other related travel. In fact, some positions with larger organizations even include designated coverage areas such as those held by sales professionals in the private sector. For example, a development officer for a large national university may be responsible for keeping in touch with alumni and donors in a four-state region.

Of course, the need to travel carries both advantages and disadvantages. On the positive side, professional travel brings a change in routine and allows you to see new places, with the added benefit that most expenses are covered by the employing agency. On the negative side, travel can sometimes be stressful, and those who travel frequently may tire of constantly being on the road.

An Average Day on the Job

With such variance in levels of responsibility and organizational goals, there is probably no such thing as an "average" day on the job for a development officer. But the following schedule illustrates what one day's work might involve for an experienced development officer:

7:30 A.M. Attend breakfast meeting with a group of volunteers.

9:00 Return phone calls from previous afternoon; write thank-you letters for recent donations; edit draft copy of new brochure.

10:00 Attend staff meeting.

11:00 Read the day's mail and prepare responses; read and respond to e-mail messages; make phone calls to co-workers regarding ongoing business; sign purchase requisitions and other documents.

12:00 P.M. Attend luncheon meeting of planning committee.

1:30 Meet with corporate representatives and internal public relations staff for photo session of a contributor making a donation.

2:00 Consult supervisor about budget request.

2:30 Meet with vendor representative to review software package being considered for accounting and donor relations.

3:30 Work on draft grant proposal.

4:30 Meet with staff to review plans for upcoming golf tournament.

5:00 Catch up on reading professional publications.

5:30 End the work day.

On another day, work might not begin with a breakfast meeting but may include a dinner meeting or another evening commitment such as a board meeting or committee meeting. And many development officers work more than eight hours a day, forty hours a week. In any case, the work conducted during a given day is sure to feature a good deal of variety.

CHAPTER 4

GRANT WRITER

While the term "fund-raising" often refers to the process of seeking private donations, a related activity brings in resources in a different way. This involves the awarding of grants.

A grant is an award, usually of money, that is to be used for a specific purpose. Grants are awarded by various agencies of both the federal government and state governments, private foundations, or other organizations. Most recipients are nonprofit organizations.

Some professionals within the fund-raising area concentrate on writing proposals to obtain grant funds. Others perform related work such as grant management. In many cases, grant writing is combined with other functions in a position that incorporates several responsibilities.

Some typical job titles for grant writers and those performing duties related to grant proposal development include:

Grant Writer
Proposal Writer
Grant Program Director
Grants Manager
Director of Sponsored Programs
Program Analyst
Contracts Manager

SOURCES OF GRANT FUNDS

There are several major sources of grant funds. Private and corporate foundations award many grants. Large foundations such as the Ford Foundation and the Kellogg Foundation award grants to nonprofit organizations in both North America and abroad.

State government agencies are another source of grant funds. These agencies often disperse large amounts of money to those who receive grants on a competitive basis.

For sheer volume of grant activity, the U.S. government would be hard to beat. The federal government awards billions of dollars annually in grant awards for a wide range of purposes. Typically, this is done through programs enacted by Congress to help solve perceived societal problems. For example, Senators and members of the House of Representatives may believe that too many children are failing to develop proper reading skills. To help address this problem, they propose a means that will provide funds for programs designed to improve the reading abilities of youngsters. Congress creates this program and authorizes funds, and the U.S. Department of Education implements it. The department sets up a grant program and allows school districts, colleges, local government agencies, and others from around the United States to apply by submitting grant applications.

Similar programs are managed by a variety of government agencies. Here is a list of some of the scores of U.S. government agencies that make grant or contract awards.

Department of Agriculture, including:

Agricultural Research Service
Economic Research Service
Farm Service Agency
Food and Nutrition Service
Food Safety and Inspection Service
Forest Service

National Agricultural Statistics Service
Natural Resources Conservation Service
Rural Housing Service
Rural Utilities Service

Department of Commerce, including:

Bureau of the Census
Economics and Statistics Administration
International Trade Administration
Bureau of Export Administration
Economic Development Administration
National Oceanic and Atmospheric Administration
National Telecommunications and Information Administration
National Institute of Standards and Technology
National Technical Information Service
Minority Business Development Agency

Department of Defense, including:

Defense Logistics Agency
U.S. Army Medical Command
Office of the Assistant Secretary (Strategy and Requirements)
Office of Economic Adjustment
Office of the Secretary
Secretaries of Military Departments
Office of the Air Force, Materiel Command
National Security Agency
Defense Advanced Research Projects Agency

Department of Housing and Urban Development, including:

Office of Community Planning and Development
Office of Fair Housing and Equal Opportunity
Office of Policy Development and Research
Office of Public and Indian Housing
Office of Lead Hazard Control

Department of the Interior, including:

Bureau of Indian Affairs

Bureau of Land Management
Office of Surface Mining Reclamation and Enforcement
Bureau of Reclamation
U.S. Fish and Wildlife Service
U.S. Geological Survey
National Park Service

Department of Justice, including:

Drug Enforcement Administration
Civil Rights Division
Community Relations Service
Immigration and Naturalization Service
Violence Against Women Office
Office of Justice Programs
Office of Juvenile Justice and Delinquency Prevention
National Institute of Justice
Bureau of Justice Assistance
Bureau of Prisons

Department of Labor, including:

Bureau of Labor Statistics
Pension and Welfare Benefits Administration
Employment and Training Administration
Employment Standards Administration
Occupational Safety and Health Administration
Mine Safety and Health Administration
Office of the Secretary, Women's Bureau
Office of the Assistant Secretary for Veterans' Employment and
    Training

Department of State, including:

Bureau of Oceans and International Environmental and Scientific Affairs
Bureau of Intelligence and Research

Department of Transportation, including:

United States Coast Guard

Federal Aviation Administration
Federal Highway Administration
Federal Railroad Administration
Federal Transit Administration
National Highway Traffic Safety Administration
Research and Special Programs Administration
Maritime Administration

Department of Treasury, including:

Under Secretary for Domestic Finance
Bureau of Alcohol, Tobacco and Firearms

Department of Health and Human Services, including:

The Administration on Aging
The Administration for Children and Families
The Administration for Children, Youth, and Families
The Administration on Developmental Disabilities
The Administration for Native Americans
The Office of Child Support Enforcement
The Office of Community Services
The Office of Family Assistance
Health Care Financing Administration
Food and Drug Administration
Centers for Disease Control
Health Resources and Services Administration
National Institutes of Health

Other U.S. government agencies awarding grants or contracts include:

Appalachian Regional Commission
National Aeronautics and Space Administration
National Foundation of Arts and the Humanities
National Science Foundation
Small Business Administration

Department of Veterans' Affairs
Environmental Protection Agency
Department of Energy
U.S. Information Agency
Federal Emergency Management Agency
Department of Education
Corporation for National and Community Service

If you have ever wondered where all that tax money goes, here is a big chunk of it! From a citizen's viewpoint you might complain about waste, or you may approve of this type of public funding. In either case, the bottom line from the viewpoint of an aggressive nonprofit organization is this: Grant money is out there for the taking.

THE GRANT MAKING PROCESS

Generally, the grant making process involves some combination of the following steps (with some variations depending on the requirements of the funding organization):

1. An agency or other organization announces that it will accept applications for grant awards. Usually this includes the publication of application materials explaining what topics applications should address, what information must be provided in an application or proposal, and who is eligible to apply. Generally a deadline date is also included beyond which applications will not be accepted (although some programs have rolling deadlines or open submission policies).
2. Potential applicants obtain an RFP (request for proposals) or application packet. This will include application instructions, forms, and related materials. It may come by mail if the applicant is already on a mailing list to receive such information.

Or, it may be sent in response to a letter, phone call, or e-mail request. Increasingly, application materials are being made available via the Internet, and interested parties may download and print copies at their discretion. Some organizations also allow proposals to be submitted via electronic means rather than the traditional submission of written proposals by mail or delivery service.

3. Staff at the applicant organization review the application materials and decide whether to submit a proposal.

4. If the decision is made to submit a proposal, one or more writers will take on the responsibility of developing the proposal. Depending on the guidelines, this might consist of a brief application just a few pages long, or it could be a proposal requiring one hundred or more pages of work.

   This is where the grant writing specialist makes his or her most important contribution. The work may performed by a staff member who focuses exclusively on grant proposal development, or by someone who also performs other fund-raising duties but includes grant writing as one set of responsibilities.

5. The writer (and others who cooperate in this process if multiple staff are involved) develops one or more drafts of the proposal. This process might take hours, days, or weeks depending on the complexity of the proposal and the time available to work on it. The writing process may include creating blocks of narrative; developing charts, graphs, and other supporting material; filling out forms; and developing budgets.

6. As the proposal is fleshed out and refined, the writer may seek input from others in the organization to see that the objectives it plans to achieve are consistent with organizational needs and existing practices.

7. When the proposal is completed, the writer obtains internal approvals as needed, including the signature of an official authorized to commit the organization to carrying out the proposed activities if the application is funded.

8. The writer sends the completed proposal (often in multiple copies) to the funding organization. Often this step is completed by clerical staff with supervision by the grant writer.

9. The funding organization reviews the proposal and evaluates it for possible approval. With many grant programs, this is a highly analytical process involving peer review. For example, one major federal program assigns three-person teams to read, evaluate, and assign scores of 0 to 100 for each proposal submitted. Out of 500 to 600 proposals submitted annually under this program, between 40 and 60 receive funding. With some other programs, the odds of success may be greater.

10. Once decisions are made, successful applicants receive an award letter. A specific funding period is established, and the applicant begins implementing the activities described in the proposal.

11. If the proposal is not funded, the writer may re-submit it the next time the agency accepts applications. The writer also may revise it to meet the requirements of other funding agencies or organizations and submit variations of the initial application accordingly. In the process, the writer may obtain copies of the ratings made by those who reviewed it (a right accorded by all federal agencies) and use them in making modifications in future versions of the proposal.

12. After this cycle is completed, or perhaps concurrently during the application process, the writer may develop other proposals for submission to different funding agencies.

Steps such as these are routine in the everyday work performed by grant writers. The details may vary, but the overall job is likely to consist of these kinds of tasks. (For tips on grant proposal development, see Appendix B.)

NEED FOR GRANT WRITERS

The process described above is a labor-intensive one. It takes a great deal of time to research, plan, and write a grant proposal. At the same time, the person doing this work must be capable of writing clearly and persuasively.

When these factors are considered together, it is easy to see that writing grants is not for everyone. Nonetheless, the specialized nature of the work involved means there is a place for those who are willing and able to perform it. Senior managers sometimes take on this responsibility for themselves, but more typically they prefer to delegate it to others. Thus in many nonprofit organizations, the position of grant writer is held by an individual who can help bring in grant funds.

DUTIES PERFORMED

What do grant writers actually do? Of course they write grant proposals, but just what does the overall job entail? Although duties vary, grant writers tend to perform some or all of the following tasks:

- research possible grant sources
- communicate with officials of grant making agencies
- develop grant proposals in their entirety from the development of rough drafts to completion of final proposals

- collect data for use in completing grant applications
- coordinate internal efforts related to grant acquisition and management
- manage funded grant projects
- evaluate the success of funded activities
- complete reports about successful grant projects
- re-write and re-submit unsuccessful grant proposals
- maintain project files
- supervise clerical staff

Often, the position of grant writer includes management responsibilities. Here is an example of a position as Director of Grants and Contracts in a community college:

Responsibilities:

— Provide leadership for the college's office of grants and contracts.
— Secure external funds to support the college's mission and goals.
— Work collaboratively across the college to develop ideas for grant projects.
— Identity and obtain funding to support a broad range of activities such as acquisition of capital equipment, student recruitment, retention and success, professional development, curriculum and instructional materials development, and other initiatives that address college goals.
— Provide leadership in refining internal processes for proposal development, review, and implementation.
— Supervise clerical staff.

Reporting: The position reports to the Director of Institutional Advancement.

Qualifications:

— Bachelor's degree (master's degree preferred).

— Three years of progressively responsible experience securing grants in an academic or not-for-profit setting.
— Demonstrated leadership and project development skills.
— Administrative and computer skills.
— Proven ability to identify funding sources that support college goals.
— Ability to present funding opportunities to senior management, faculty, and staff and engage in active participation in resource development projects.
— Capability of collaborating with senior management, faculty, and staff to develop competitive grant projects.
— Ability to direct and supervise the preparation of college proposals that result in the acquisition of external funds.
— Ability to monitor grant projects from start-up to project completion.

To illustrate the expectations for another such position, what follows is an example of a description for a grants management position at a nonprofit organization dedicated to exploring public policy issues:

Position Title: Grants Manager

Responsibilities:

— Managing all aspects of the grant process.
— Researching, writing, and following up on all proposals.
— Working closely with the administrative staff to ensure that all communications accurately reflect the organization's mission, policies, and programs.
— Coordinating financial information to ensure accuracy in financial reporting.
— Managing scheduling process and ensuring timely submission of proposals and reports.
— Conducting research on existing and potential funders.
— Assisting in stewardship of funders.

Qualifications:

— College degree.

— Three to four years' experience as a grants writer.
— Ability to gather, analyze, and synthesize information.
— Ability to prepare coherent and compelling proposals as well as other materials such as reports and letters.
— Experience using research tools.
— Strong administrative and organizational skills.
— Excellent written communication skills with ability to communicate effectively.
— Computer literacy with proficiency in word processing and fund management software.

ACQUIRING GRANT WRITING SKILLS

There is no specific set of requirements that must be met to become a grant writer. Many people participate in a kind of on-the-job training process where they learn by obtaining an RFP or grant application booklet, following the instructions, and developing their first proposal. After doing this several times and interacting with others in the process, many writers become competent grant writers.

Those who intend to focus on this area, however, usually benefit by participating in some formal instruction on the subject. This may consist of a grant writing course taken as a part of an undergraduate or graduate program (see Chapter 7 for examples). Or, it may involve attending a short-term seminar or workshop. Instead of a college course lasting a semester or more, this usually takes only a few days, or in some cases, a day or less. Of course, the amount of material that can be covered is a function of the time devoted to the subject, but short-term training of this type can still be a great way to develop and enhance a basic understanding of grant writing techniques.

For example, the Foundation Center, headquartered in New York City, offers seminars around the country on grant writing.

Most of those who attend are employees of nonprofit organizations who want to develop or improve their grant writing skills. But students and others who want to develop such skills also may participate.

Typical seminar topics include the following:

- winning proposal-writing techniques
- essential components of grant proposals
- fine tuning proposals to match the interests of grant makers
- following through after proposals have been submitted
- keeping up with trends in grant making

For more information, contact the Foundation Center at 79 Fifth Avenue, New York, NY 10003.

TRAITS NEEDED FOR SUCCESS IN GRANT WRITING

In addition to general requirements (such as, in most cases, the minimum of a bachelor's degree), successful grant writers need certain traits. These include some or most of the following:

1. Excellent writing skills (including not just basic writing ability, but the ability to create, organize, and present material in a cogent, persuasive manner).
2. Excellent editing and proofreading skills.
3. Enthusiasm in taking on projects and seeing them through to their completion.
4. A high energy level and the willingness to work long hours if necessary to complete a project.
5. The ability to meet deadlines.
6. The ability to accept criticism and learn from disappointments.
7. Creativity and problem-solving ability.
8. Good analytical skills.
9. The ability to work cooperatively with others.

10. A willingness to take risks in project development.
11. The ability to use word processing to create documents.
12. Persistence in carrying out work tasks.

Questions to Ask Yourself

If the possibility of working as a grant writer appeals to you, ask yourself questions such as these:

- Do I enjoy developing written materials?
- Do I have excellent skills in grammar, mechanics, organization, and other elements of the writing process? Do others consider me a talented writer?
- Would I be comfortable sitting for long periods of time working on writing proposals?
- Can I work well without a great deal of direct supervision?
- Would I be comfortable having my work rated by reviewers and continuously evaluated in competition with the work of others?
- Am I willing to obtain the necessary training or academic preparation to prepare for a job in this field?
- Am I good at using a personal computer or other office equipment?
- Can I work well with others?
- Am I good at meeting deadlines? Can I tolerate the stress involved in meeting frequent deadlines?

If most of your answers are in the affirmative, working as a grant writer may be a possibility for you. To investigate further, take a class in grant writing or attend a noncredit seminar as mentioned previously. Another possibility is to obtain some sample RFPs for government-sponsored grant programs, look through them, and perhaps develop a draft proposal as a class project or personal undertaking.

Also keep in mind that RFPs, successful grant proposals, and other documents are often in the public domain and may be free on request from government agencies. A good place to start is your local congressperson's office. You can also check out websites of government agencies and go from there.

CHAPTER 5

PLANNED GIVING SPECIALIST

An important trend in the world of fund-raising is a growing interest in the concept of planned giving. This is the practice of combining elements of financial planning and philanthropy while taking tax considerations into account. Put more simply, planned giving provides people a way of planning ahead to make charitable donations that reduce the amount of taxes they or their families must pay to the government. Usually this is done in a way that benefits both the donor (or the donor's family) and the recipient, while at the same time limiting tax payments in a fully legal and respectable manner.

THE TRANSFER OF WEALTH

A significant development that has fueled the growth of planned giving programs is the so-called "transfer of wealth" from one generation to the next. Although there is nothing new about people inheriting wealth from their parents or other relatives, shifts in population and economic growth have combined to bring on an unprecedented situation where the volume of money transferring hands from one generation to the next is larger than ever before.

According to a Boston College study reported in *USA Today,* somewhere between twelve and eighteen *trillion* dollars will be passed from one generation to the next in the period that began in 1998 and extends through 2017! This is due primarily to the deaths of the parents of a huge population of "baby boomers" (those born in the population boom following World War II), along with other deaths occurring naturally in the growing population of North America and the resultant inheritance process.

Just how does this affect fund-raising? Two basic factors come into play. First is the natural desire of people to share their wealth with causes in which they believe. In making out wills or taking out life insurance policies, people often include schools, churches, charities, or other organizations to receive some of their inheritance.

Second is the way that taxes are assessed. In the United States, the federal government levies heavy taxes on estates of a certain size. In larger estates, anywhere from 18 to 55 percent (or more, in very large estates) of the money left behind is taken for taxes. Yet tax laws include provisions that reduce tax liability when certain types of donations are made. This includes situations in which nonprofit organizations may receive gifts during the lifetimes of donors instead of after their deaths. These arrangements can become what may be called "win-win" situations, in which the donor and the recipient of donations such as land, stock, and so forth both benefit from the transaction.

THE BASICS OF PLANNED GIVING

According to information provided to potential donors by Clark University, planned giving actually consists of two distinct components: planning and giving. While giving is obviously the most important factor, prior planning can make it more effective. This refers to the consideration of estate planning, financial planning, and tax planning by a donor before making a gift. Thus planned giving deals with three general circumstances:

1. An outright gift that might consist of stock, tangible personal property, or real estate, among other possibilities, with the recipient usually having immediate access to the donation.
2. A bequest that does not actually go to the recipient until after the donor has died.
3. What is known as a life income gift, in which a donor makes a gift but still receives income from it even though ownership has been transferred to the nonprofit organization receiving the gift.

A simple type of planned giving is to take out a life insurance policy with a nonprofit organization as the beneficiary instead of a family member. For example, an alumnus of a college might take out a $100,000 life insurance policy with the college named as a beneficiary. The alumnus pays the premiums, and then at his or her death, the college receives the money, which will be used as specified by the donor. He or she may want the funds to go toward scholarships, library books, athletics, or an unrestricted purpose. Whatever use the donor stipulated the college will follow as a matter of ethical practice.

Overseeing this process is the responsibility of fund-raising professionals employed by the college. They may confer with the donor when the policy is first taken out, but even if not, they will be responsible for accepting the gift and then investing or spending the funds according to the donor's wishes.

More complex types of planned giving entail the same types of responsibilities on the part of fund-raising professionals. In addition, they necessitate special training and knowledge.

For example, several types of trusts may be used as planned giving vehicles. They involve specific legal obligations on the part of each party involved, and it is the responsibility of planned giving officers to coordinate the process of developing and entering into such agreements with donors. Of course, the decision to make such a donation rests with the donor, but helping people with such decisions and coordinating their implementation is the responsibility of planned giving officers.

DUTIES OF PLANNED GIVING SPECIALISTS

Professionals who work in planned giving may have a variety of titles, such as the following:

Director of Planned Giving
Associate Director of Planned Giving
Planned Giving Officer
Planned Giving Specialist
Director of Major Gifts and Planned Giving

Most professionals who specialize in this area perform some or all of the following functions:

- solicit planned gifts from potential donors
- develop documents related to the planned giving process
- coordinate the involvement of attorneys, accountants, bankers, or others in the planned giving process
- coordinate the marketing and management of planned giving programs
- create plans for planned giving activities
- develop and implement marketing plans for planned giving programs
- locate and contact potential donors
- accept and acknowledge gifts
- provide information to potential donors including referrals to specialists
- coordinate memorial gift programs or other activities

- educate prospective donors about planned giving opportunities and the processes involved
- evaluate planned giving programs and activities
- conduct one-on-one meetings with donors or potential donors
- arrange or coordinate group meetings with those involved in a planned giving transaction
- write letters, memos, reports, and promotional materials
- maintain documents related to planned giving
- ensure that ethical practices are followed in all activities related to the planned giving process

Planned giving specialists need not necessarily be attorneys or accountants, but they must be able to communicate effectively with these types of professionals as well as with bank trust officers, other experts, and potential donors. This means, among other things, that they must be able to "speak the lingo" involved and should have a broad-based understanding not only of planned giving options, but also of more general terms and practices.

For example, a prospective donor who has done well in the stock market may want to discuss the possibility of donating stocks as part of a planned giving arrangement. In communicating about this possibility, general comments about the current state of the stock market may come up. In such instances, the planned giving officer will be expected to understand the terms and concepts involved.

Similarly, the ability to discuss concepts related to wills, insurance, and tax implications is necessary in general, if not specific, terms. Of course, if a planned giving officer has a background as an attorney, trust officer, or other specialist, so much the better. But even without such background, a professional in this field must have a basic understanding of terminology, concepts, and practical implications of all aspects of the planned giving process.

Equally important, planned giving officers must be conversant in the issues addressed by the agency employing them. This means that while they serve as specialists, they also function as overall representatives of the organization. A college planned giving officer, for instance, should be able to discuss with donors and others the latest challenges faced by the institution, plans for the future, and so forth.

Here is an example of a description for a planned giving position at a private four-year college:

Job Title: Director of Planned Giving

Overall Responsibilities:

— Work with administrative staff, faculty, and other development staff to promote planned giving.
— Identify and cultivate donor prospects.
— Provide stewardship for persons who have entered into planned giving contracts.

Specific Duties:

— Identify prospects who may be interested in contributing through the planned giving process.
— Manage a budget and travel schedule that facilitates ten to twenty prospect visits per month.
— Negotiate and close a wide range of planned giving arrangements including charitable gift annuities, charitable remainder and lead trusts, pooled income fund gifts, testamentary trusts, life insurance policies, and retained life estates.
— Provide stewardship for holders of planned giving contracts through letters, newsletters, visits, recognition activities, and other means.
— Conduct a comprehensive marketing program for the plan including arranging for educational seminars for a wide range of constituents.

— Assist in establishing goals, objectives, and strategies for the planned giving program.
— Participate in assessing progress toward meeting goals, including submitting monthly progress reports.
— Participate in training and professional development activities as needed to remain up to date in knowledge of planned giving issues and vehicles.

Qualifications:

— Bachelor's degree required with advanced degree in law, tax, or other related field preferred; previous service in planned giving or experience in an allied field such as legal, tax, or financial planning preferred.
— Ability to work closely and congenially with other personnel and with volunteers.
— Ability to communicate effectively with others.
— Ability and willingness to travel and attend meetings and functions at various hours as needed.
— Knowledge of planned giving vehicles including charitable gift annuities, charitable remainder and lead trusts, pooled income fund gifts, testamentary trusts, life insurance policies, and retained life estates.
— Knowledge of estate planning and federal tax law as applied to charitable giving.
— Ability to work in a fast-paced environment with numerous deadlines and pressures.
— Ability to operate or oversee the operation of computers to prepare reports and other written documents using word processing, spreadsheets, and database and graphics programs.
— Excellent verbal and writing skills, including the ability to determine relevant information, form compelling cases for support, and digest and synthesize large quantities of information into a few paragraphs when necessary.
— Ability to work with a high degree of flexibility, accuracy, and attention to detail.

The following description covers a similar position at another institution:

Position: Director of Planned Giving/Major Gifts

Responsibilities:

— Build and maintain active cultivation and solicitation of prospects for planned gifts.
— Maintain knowledge of planned giving vehicles.
— Solicit annual, campaign, and planned gifts.
— Produce and maintain an energetic marketing campaign to initiate interest in planned gifts.
— Organize and participate in cultivation events.
— Utilize planned gift software to assist donors in understanding the personal advantages of planned giving instruments for the benefit of the university.
— Formulate strategies for prospects who will be cultivated and solicited by the vice presidents, president, and trustees.
— Plan and manage budget and development goals.
— Participate in development projects as assigned by the vice president.
— Travel as needed.

Qualifications:

— Bachelor's degree required; advanced degree preferred.
— Two to four years of major gifts/planned gifts or trust officer experience with demonstrated ability to market, solicit, and close major gifts/planned gifts.
— Enthusiasm for direct, regular, ongoing personal interaction with donors and prospects.
— Exceptional communication skills, including the ability to write clear and compelling correspondence and conduct effective one-on-one presentations.
— Ability to work in an office where teamwork and professional respect are the foundation for achievement.

SPECIALIZED KNOWLEDGE

To a greater degree than in some other fund-raising areas, those who work in planned giving need specialized job knowledge. Whether obtained through formal training or developed through on-the-job experience, this will include familiarity with concepts and practices such as the following:

- dealing with gifts comprising noncash assets
- understanding and communicating applications of wills and trusts in making or receiving planned gifts
- identifying strengths and weaknesses of different types of planned giving vehicles such as charitable remainder trusts, revocable living trusts, and charitable lead trusts
- understanding tax implications of strategies for making planned gifts
- understanding advantages of annuities and life insurance policies

How does one gain such specialized knowledge? One approach is to participate in seminars or institutes covering the basics of planned giving.

Perhaps the leading provider of such training is the National Planned Giving Institute at the College of William and Mary in Williamsburg, Virginia, which consists of a series of eight comprehensive seminars on planned giving and related areas. These seminars help participants develop skills in planning, marketing, managing, and evaluating efforts to develop planned gifts, as well as to sharpen related skills.

A look at the eight seminar areas can be illustrative in several ways. Not only does it provide an example of a well-designed plan for educational preparation in this area, but a review of the topics covered can give you a good idea of the many facets of the work involved in a staff position responsible for planned giving efforts.

SEMINAR #1: PLANNING, MARKETING, MANAGING, AND EVALUATING YOUR PLANNED GIVING PROGRAM

Topics include:

Perspectives on Planned Giving

The Fund-Raising Circles and Models

How a Donor-Driven Approach Can Increase Your Planned Gifts

The Life Cycle of a Donor—Managing the Transition from Current to Deferred Gifts

Planning Your Planned Giving Program

Marketing, Managing, and Evaluating Your Planned Giving Program Gift Acceptance Policies

How Informed Trustees and Senior Staff Can Make Planned Giving Efforts More Productive

Ethical Considerations in Planned Giving

Overview of the Plans of Giving

SEMINAR #2: INFORMING, MOTIVATING, AND EDUCATING PROSPECTIVE PLANNED GIVERS

Topics include:

Positioning Your Institution in the Minds of Givers—Who Are You?

Identifying and Researching Prospects—Who Are They?

Broad-Based Marketing Approaches

How to Use Target Marketing to Discover Planned Gift Prospects

Communication Techniques You Can Use to Find Hidden Planned Gift Prospects

How to Qualify and Disqualify Prospective Planned Givers

Interviewing Prospective Givers

How Your Donor and Prospect Tracking Systems Work for You

Establishing a Recognition and Memorial Gifts Program

Group Communication Approaches to Help Secure Planned Gifts

Seven Ways to Start Increasing Planned Gifts

Charting a Marketing Course

SEMINAR #3: FUNDING MAJOR CURRENT AND DEFERRED PLANNED GIFTS WITH NONCASH PROPERTIES

Topics include:

Securing Major Current and Deferred Planned Gifts from Noncash Assets

Discovering the Property People Own and How to Help Them Give It

An Introduction to Property and Forms of Ownership

When Foundation and Corporate Gifts Result from Major Gift Activities

How to Fund Major Current and Deferred Planned Gifts with Real Estate or Securities

Major Gifts from Retirement Plan Property

Major Current and Deferred Gifts of Life Insurance and Annuity Policies

Gifts of Other Contract Assets

Understanding Forms of Business Ownership and Private Foundations

What You Need to Know About Valuing Noncash Gifts and IRS-Required Appraisals

How to Transfer Tangible and Intangible Personal Property— Review of Tax Consequences

SEMINAR #4: TAXES AND GIVING

Topics include:

An Introduction to Federal Income Tax Effects of Charitable Gifts by Individuals and Corporations

Taxation of Gifts of Cash, Securities, Real Property, Ordinary
Income Property, Tangible and Intangible Personal Property,
Bargain Sales, and Gifts of Mortgaged Property

Tax Implications of Charitable Remainder Annuity Trusts and
Charitable Remainder Unitrusts; Pooled Income Funds and
Charitable Lead Trusts; Bequests, Revocable Living Trusts,
Charitable Gift Annuities, and Life Estate Contracts

Analyzing the Cost of Charitable Giving through Tax Savings

Using Tax Incentives to Increase Charitable Gifts

Using Marketing and Tax Strategies to Help Secure Current and
Deferred Major Planned Gifts

Case Studies and Workshops

SEMINAR #5: THE NONINCOME TAX–ORIENTED PLANS OF GIVING

Topics include:

Understanding What You Need to Know about Wills

How Communicating Wills Information Can Lead to Bequests

How Wills Awareness Programs Lead to Other Planned Gifts

How You and Your Attorney Can Conduct a Wills Clinic

Deferred Gift Potential from Retirement Assets and Life Insurance and Annuity Policies

Revocable Living Trusts

A Review of Revocable Plans of Giving

Understanding Life Estate Arrangements

Understanding Gift Annuities

Deferred Gift Potential from Contractual Assets

SEMINAR #6: THE INCOME TAX–ORIENTED PLANS OF GIVING

Topics include:

Understanding the Trust Concept—Testamentary vs. *Inter Vivos*
(living)

Charitable Remainder Annuity Trusts and Unitrusts

Pooled Income Plans
Charitable Lead Trust
Gift Substantiation and Disclosure Rules
Gaining Support from Your Chief Financial Officer
Working with Major Gift Prospects
How You Can Help Investment Managers and Trustees Help
    You
Working with Allied Professionals
Understanding the Time Value of Money
Which Planned Gift Arrangement Meets Your Donors' Needs

The seventh and eighth seminars in this series focus on building future gift income through charitable estate and gift planning.

For information contact the institute at:

National Planned Giving Institute
    The College of William and Mary
    P.O. Box 8795
    Williamsburg, VA 23187

Other educational opportunities cover similar content, although not necessarily in this much detail. Some are offered by professional associations serving those employed in fund-raising, such as the National Society of Fund Raising Executives, the Council for Resource Development, or the Council for Advancement and Support of Education. Others are sponsored by consulting firms that specialize in fund-raising, training, or both.

You can identity such opportunities by checking with professional organizations or perusing publications such as the *Chronicle of Philanthropy* or the *Non-Profit Times* (see later chapters on education and professional associations for more details). You also can learn by reading books and periodical articles in planned giving topics (see Appendix A for several book listings).

A publication of possible interest is *Planned Giving Today,* a newsletter serving charitable gift planners in the United States and Canada. This newsletter provides news, educational articles, and other information including a supplement that lists employment opportunities.

For more information write to:

Planned Giving Today
100 Second Avenue South
Edmonds, WA 98020

ADVANTAGES AND DISADVANTAGES

The advantages and disadvantages of a career in planned giving are similar to those of other fund-raising positions, but with some special considerations. Advantages include:

- The opportunity to perform work that supports the mission of a nonprofit organization is truly helpful to people
- You will have the chance to provide a service to individuals who need assistance in directing their charitable contributions toward appropriate causes.
- There is the challenge of performing complex work that requires a substantial knowledge base and a high level of proficiency.
- You will have the opportunity to work in a stimulating workplace such as a college, charitable organization, or other such environment.
- With experience, you will develop skills that can be transferred to other career areas.

Disadvantages may include some or all of the following:

- With the specialized nature of this type of work, job openings at any given time in a specific geographical area or within a given type of nonprofit organization may be limited.

- In some positions the job may be quite stressful, especially where the circumstances involve meeting ambitious goals.
- Dealing with potential donors can be demanding in a number of ways.
- Extensive travel may be required. This can also be an advantage, but in some cases, frequent travel may be regarded as an inconvenience that disrupts one's everyday personal life.

TRAITS NEEDED FOR A CAREER IN PLANNED GIVING

The skills needed to work in planned giving are similar to those needed in other areas of fund-raising. Specifically they include some or all of the following:

- excellent skills in written and oral communications
- the ability to communicate with people in a manner that they find nonthreatening and trustworthy
- analytical ability, including the ability to work with charts, graphs, and presentation materials
- a high level of energy and enthusiasm for the work
- a strong sense of commitment to the employing organization
- high moral standards and personal ethics
- the patience to move slowly as potential donors make decisions about planned giving options
- the ability to communicate effectively with specialists such as attorneys or tax experts
- an understanding of the importance of teamwork
- a strong work ethic including good organizational and follow-up skills

Questions to Ask Yourself

In considering the possibility of a planned giving career, ask yourself these questions:

- Do I enjoy working with people in one-on-one or small group settings?
- Do I have good oral communication skills? Solid writing skills?
- Would I be comfortable discussing people's estate plans and encouraging them to make substantial contributions of money or other resources?
- Am I good at working with details?
- Do I work well without a great deal of direct supervision?
- Am I willing to travel extensively if that is a job requirement?
- Would I be comfortable working as a specialist who is part of a larger team of fund-raising professionals?
- Am I willing to obtain specialized training to gain skills and knowledge in the planned giving area?
- Am I good at following through on details and keeping accurate records?
- Do I have the right kind of personality to "sell" the needs of a nonprofit organization to donors or potential donors?

An affirmative answer to most or all of these questions is desirable if you are serious about working in the planned giving arena. For the right individuals, this can be one of the most rewarding types of fund-raising careers.

CHAPTER 6

FUND-RAISING SUPPORT JOBS

The process of raising funds and generating external support is a complex one. In addition to broad-based jobs such as those performed by development directors, a number of specialized career areas support fund-raising or are related to such efforts.

Such positions can provide an avenue to other related jobs, or they can offer their own distinct career paths. The following is a brief overview of some positions.

RESEARCH SPECIALIST

The typical image of a successful fund-raiser is probably that of a "people person," or someone who relishes meeting new people, enjoys making conversation, and is adept at handling social situations. While that is often the case, it is not always the required personality profile to succeed in the fund-raising field. There is also a place for those who work in the background. Such is the case for workers who specialize in prospect research and related functions.

Prospect research involves the process of identifying possible donors. Prospect researchers address questions such as these: Who would be likely to donate funds to our organization? Who has large amounts of resources that might allow them to make substantial gifts? What possible interests or ties could we identify that would

65

link an individual or corporation to our organization and the causes we serve?

Those who work in prospect research find answers to such questions. They use reading, writing, and research skills to gather and organize data in support of fund-raising programs.

Typically such a position requires a college degree, with previous development research experience providing an inside track to job applicants. The ability to utilize various business and financial sources is a must, along with proficiency in word processing and in using the Internet as a research tool. An understanding of database management applications and electronic screening tools and experience in evaluating sources are helpful. Well-developed research, analytical, writing, and communication skills also are needed.

A typical position of this type includes activities in prospect management, prospect identification, and maintenance of donor research. It may also include tasks such as supervising research staff and performing strategic analyses for individual and institutional donors.

Following is a description of a research position at the University of Virginia, a public university that operates an extensive fund-raising program:

Position Title: Development Program Researcher

Duties:

— Conduct extensive research to locate prospective donors to provide funds for the University of Virginia.
— Compile, analyze, and verify biographical and financial information.
— Establish and maintain filing systems.
— Develop comprehensive reports on potential individual, corporate, and foundation donors.

Qualifications:

— B.S. or B.A. degree with course work in research principles, writing, communications, marketing, library sciences, or related fields. An equivalent combination of experience/training may substitute for education.
— Ability to communicate effectively both orally and in writing.
— Ability to research and analyze a variety of reference materials.
— Ability to word process and to effectively use electronic databases as resource tools.

While the previous position might be regarded as an entry-level assignment, the following position holds a greater range of responsibilities. After serving in the lower-level job, a successful worker might advance to this classification.

Position title: Development Program Researcher Senior

Position Description:

— Serve as a charge position for a development/fund-raising research unit.
— Plan, organize, and conduct research; review or develop solicitation strategy recommendations and participate in development/fund-raising strategic planning.
— Analyze and evaluate financial, statistical, and narrative documents to compile research data and determine a targeted prospect's available resources and interests.
— Construct and test methods of data collection; write reports for use by executives and other development managers; review and make suggestions to improve quality of bibliographical profiles, research data, reports, and solicitation strategies to upper management; and participate in agencywide development planning.
— Hire, train, and evaluate staff.

Qualifications:

— Bachelor's degree and considerable experience as a development program researcher, preferably in a higher education institution.
— Demonstrated ability to communicate effectively both orally and in writing, to research and analyze a variety of reference materials, and to use electronic databases as resource tools.
— Prior management experience preferred.

Here is an example of a position description for a Prospect Research Officer at a smaller four-year college:

Qualifications:

— Bachelor's degree required along with at least two years of experience in research of individuals, corporations, and foundations. Experience in higher education research preferred. Must be proficient in the use of database systems, the Internet, and online corporate/foundation and biographical resources.

Duties:

— Research individual alumni prospects as identified by board members, college administrative staff, and others.
— Research information about corporations, foundations, and other potential donor organizations.
— Research and identify prospective donors through mailings, newspaper articles, clipping services, verbal leads, and other sources.
— Assist in maintaining and updating the development office's research library, including both hard-copy resources and subscriptions to online research services.
— Assist in maintaining information about alumni, donors, and potential donors.
— Complete reports based on a variety of research techniques and maintain prospect files.

Reporting: The position reports to the college's Director of Development.

Unlike most other positions related to fund-raising, research-based positions provide opportunities for those who are interested in being a part of the overall development team, but who enjoy completing analytical work more than engaging in social interaction. A typical day on the job may be spent working at a computer, combing through written records or preparing documentation for review by other members of the fund-raising team.

Jobs in this area of research are more commonly found at larger organizations, which have the resources to support a diverse fund-raising staff. At smaller organizations, such duties may be combined with other responsibilities or assigned in a limited fashion to clerical support staff.

SPECIAL EVENTS COORDINATOR

Most nonprofit organizations use special events as tools to support fund-raising. In some cases the primary purpose of such an event is to generate donations. For example, an organization may sponsor a golf tournament or an art auction with the proceeds going to support its fund-raising objectives.

Other special events focus on donor relations or overall public exposure rather than fund-raising in a strict sense. An event such as the dedication of a new building, the unveiling of a recently acquired painting, or a reception to welcome new board members may be held for groups of varying sizes.

Coordinating such events, along with other responsibilities, is often a duty handled by a development officer, but it can also form the basis for a position dedicated to coordinating or managing such events. Some organizations employ special events coordinators (also known as special events managers or some similar title) for this purpose.

Typical duties for this type of position include:

- planning special events
- coordinating events from the planning stage through their completion
- assisting in maintaining positive relations with donors, potential donors, and others
- evaluating the effectiveness of special events
- managing budgets related to event programming
- supervising support staff

The background and skills needed for this function are similar to those required of a more broad-based development position. In addition, success in special events requires a solid understanding of etiquette and mastery of what might be called the social graces. An eye for detail and excellent planning skills are also needed.

CLERICAL OR OFFICE SUPPORT STAFF

Employees who perform clerical or office support functions also contribute in important ways to fund-raising activities. Typically these positions do not lead to higher level management positions or direct fund-raising jobs, but it is possible to use such jobs as stepping-stones to other fund-raising jobs or related roles.

In smaller offices, secretaries or administrative assistants may perform some tasks that might be handled by other personnel in larger organizations. This can provide experience in fund-raising that might be used to gain competencies that eventually form the basis for advancing to other jobs in the field.

Within larger organizations, on-the-job experience also might lead to consideration for promotion to a higher-level job. This is more likely if the experience is complemented by completion of college classes, attendance at noncredit seminars, or other educational efforts.

Some support positions involve providing general office support such as word processing, maintaining files, handling telephone communications, and coordinating office workflow. Others focus on more specialized tasks such as maintaining financial records or supporting prospect research professionals.

Typical titles for these positions include:

Administrative Assistant
Administrative Associate
Executive Secretary
Secretary
Correspondence Secretary
Assistant to the Director
Office Manager
Office Assistant
Fiscal Technician
Word Processing Specialist
Research Assistant

One advantage of a job in this area is that it provides an opportunity to work as part of a fund-raising team without having earned a bachelor's degree or advanced degree. A one-year diploma or a two-year degree from a community college can provide the entry-level skills needed for employment in this area.

CONSULTANT

Most of the jobs detailed in this book represent ongoing staff or administrative positions. But an entirely different approach is taken by professional consultants who specialize in fund-raising or related activities. Their work is done on a contract basis rather than as permanent employees. In other words, nonprofit organizations hire consultants on a short-term basis to complete specific assignments.

An example of a common role of consultants in fund-raising is the development of a feasibility study for a fund-raising campaign. Here a consultant will help an organization look carefully at its potential to put together a large-scale fund-raising campaign. Using sophisticated information gathering techniques, the consultant provides details that are crucial to such a decision. The organization then considers this advice before making decisions about how to proceed.

Another typical activity is writing grant proposals or assisting others in the writing or editing process. Using specialized knowledge of proposal-writing techniques, as well as understanding of the programs through which funding is sought, consultants in proposal development prepare proposals or assist staff in developing them.

Consultants who assist nonprofit organizations may focus on a specific type of fund-raising, or they may have a more broad-based approach that includes other areas of expertise. Examples of areas covered by consulting firms include:

- planning and conducting capital campaigns
- direct mail marketing
- accounting systems development
- operations or facilities support
- copywriting and editing services
- database management
- mailing list development
- marketing and public relations assistance
- program evaluation
- donor recognition programs

- special events programs
- investment services
- professional development and training activities

A good source of information about consulting firms serving nonprofit organizations is the American Association of Fund-Raising Counsel. This organization provides a membership directory that is free on request, and its website includes direct links to a number of consulting firms.

For more information contact:

American Association of Fund-Raising Counsel
    www.aafrc.org

GOVERNMENT RELATIONS OFFICER

Many nonprofit organizations, such as state-supported colleges and universities, health agencies, and other organizations, receive funding directly from state legislatures, federal appropriations, or other government sources. Others that do not rely on direct government funding may benefit from grants or contracts earned on a competitive basis. Still others receive no government funds but still depend on legislation that is favorable to their organization. Thus for virtually all nonprofit organizations, it is important for staff to be knowledgeable about government actions and, in many cases, to communicate with government officials.

To address this need, nonprofit organizations often include government relations as a job duty of at least one staff member, most typically the chief development officer. Taking things further, some organizations have positions where this is the primary responsibility. These government relations officers represent the needs of the organization in dealing with state legislators, members of the U.S. Senate or House of Representatives, government agency heads, program officers, or other officials. Some deal only with officials within their own state; others deal with federal officials or a combination of the two.

Examples of such roles include:

- Mississippi State University, which employs a Government Relations Officer who works within the university's Division of External Affairs
- The University of Washington, which maintains the position of Director of Government Relations who focuses on state government contacts
- Pennsylvania's Chester County Schools, which has a Director of Government Relations who communicates with state government officials and keeps school officials informed about state and federal legislation, among other duties
- The College Board, a national nonprofit educational association, which employs a number of government relations officers (with titles such as Vice President for Government Relations and Communications or Executive Director of Federal and State Relations) and directors of regional offices

Such positions are not as common as most other jobs related to fund-raising or external support, but they do provide challenging careers for the small number of people who pursue them. These jobs entail similar work as other positions designed to foster external support, but with the additional need for an in-depth understanding of the legislative process and an ability to operate within the political or government arena.

OTHER POSITIONS

A variety of other jobs can be found that either include responsibilities for raising funds or provide support to fund-raising functions. Some examples include:

Account Executive
Call Center Manager
Tax Advisor or Tax Accountant
Public Relations Specialist
Marketing Director
Staff Attorney
Alumni Affairs Coordinator
Program Director
Direct Mail Coordinator
Executive Manager

These and other positions have their places in the nonprofit world and as such represent additional career possibilities for those interested in the broad spectrum of fund-raising and related careers.

CHAPTER 7

EDUCATIONAL PREPARATION

GENERAL BACKGROUND REQUIRED

There is no single, specific set of educational qualifications for a career in fund-raising. The most common expectation is a bachelor's degree in a liberal arts field, communications or business, or in a field related to the purposes of the employing organization. In addition, an advanced degree is expected for some positions (especially those in colleges and universities), but this may not be a requirement even in higher education settings. For some positions, an associate degree or a combination of education and experience may be sufficient for an entry-level position.

Typical college majors of those who become employed in fund-raising include the following:

English
Communications
Business Administration
Marketing
Journalism
Public Relations
Management
Economics

Public Administration
Liberal Arts or General Studies

MAKING EDUCATIONAL PLANS

Relatively few people who work in fund-raising select that career goal in high school and then pursue it from there. More typically, they discover the field while in college or after graduating from college when exploring career options. However, it is certainly possible to chart a career path in that direction. Such a plan might include the following steps:

- selecting a college
- obtaining financial aid or other resources necessary to support college attendance
- attending college, and during that process selecting an appropriate major or course of study
- gaining experience in the nonprofit sector through volunteer work, internships, part-time or summer employment, or other experiences
- participating in selected seminars, workshops, classes, or credit-based academic programs related to fund-raising skills and techniques

Choosing a College

To be eligible for the majority of jobs in fund-raising, a first step is obtaining a college degree. In selecting a college, a number of factors should be taken into account. The U.S. Department of Education suggests asking these basic questions when considering a college:

Does the school offer the courses and type of program I want?
Do I meet the admissions requirements?
Does the school offer a quality education at a reasonable price?
Does the school offer services I need and activities in which I'm interested?

The department notes that most of this information is covered in any college's catalog or in its introductory brochures and, in many cases, via the Internet, since many colleges and universities have websites. Other factors to consider include:

- opinions of friends or relatives who have previously attended the school
- evidence that the college is fully accredited
- the institution's loan default rate (that is, is the percentage of students who attended the school, took out federal student loans, and later failed to repay their loans on time)
- the college's campus security policies and campus crime statistics
- the institution's job placement rates
- the school's refund policy
- completion and transfer rates
- the availability of financial aid

If you're considering any college, be sure to visit it at least once and get a firsthand look at the campus. Also keep in mind that choosing a college is an important decision, but not necessarily a permanent one. You can always start out at one school and transfer to another. In fact, a great way to get started is to attend a community college and then transfer to a four-year college after completing a year or two of studies. But whatever your choice, keep in mind that virtually any college can provide a good educational experience if you are willing to work hard and learn as much as possible.

Paying for College

Concurrent with the process of selecting a college, it is important to explore all the options for paying for it. Attending college is more expensive than ever. You might incur costs for tuition, application fees, book costs, room and board, and commuting expenses.

Costs can total from around $1,000 to $3,000 per year at a typical community college to between $20,000 and $30,000 yearly at many private colleges, with public universities and other colleges falling somewhere between the two. With such a large investment, most students will want to pursue financial assistance.

Colleges and universities offer a variety of scholarships, grants, loans, and other types of aid. In addition, thousands of private organizations sponsor scholarships and other financial help. A smart move is to apply for multiple sources of financial assistance since most sponsoring programs are competitive in nature.

Financial aid from the federal government comes in several varieties, including the following:

Pell Grants. These are outright grants that, unlike loans, do not have to be repaid. Pell Grants may be awarded to undergraduate students who have not earned bachelors' or professional degrees. They are based on financial need, with the neediest students obtaining the largest awards.

FSEOG (Federal Supplemental Educational Opportunity Grants). These are grants for undergraduates with exceptional financial need. Pell Grant recipients with extra financial need also may receive FSEOG awards.

Federal Work-Study. This program provides part-time jobs for undergraduate and graduate students who demonstrate financial need. It provides a source of financial assistance along with the opportunity to gain work experience while still in school.

Federal Perkins Loans. These are loans for undergraduate or graduate students with exceptional financial need. They must be repaid, but because of government backing, the interest rate is lower than it is for most other types of loans.

Stafford Loans. Offered through the William D. Ford Direct Loan Program, these loans are available to students who do not obtain sufficient help from other sources, as well as those who do not necessarily have the level of need of students qualifying for other federal aid programs but who still need financial assistance. The interest rate is lower than most commercial loans, and borrowers can take a long time (up to thirty years, if desired) to repay them.

Other types of aid include PLUS loans (available to parents) as well as several other programs.

To apply for federal student aid, complete a Free Application for Federal Student Aid (FAFSA). You can apply electronically from your home computer or from a computer at a central location or submit a paper application in English or Spanish.

For more information consult the U.S. Department of Education home page at:

www.fafsa.ed.gov

Or write to:

Federal Student Aid Information Center
    P.O. Box 84
    Washington, DC 20044
    1-800-4-FED-AID (1-800-433-3243)

In addition to government aid, don't overlook the many other sources of aid available. These include scholarships offered by colleges, scholarships sponsored by various organizations, state-sponsored grants and scholarships, and other sources.

For more information about various sources of aid, consult the following:

- the U.S. Department of Education home page and other websites about financial aid and scholarships
- college financial aid offices
- high school guidance counselors
- financial aid directories available in libraries and bookstores

FROM COLLEGE TO EMPLOYMENT

Once in college, the courses taken and other experiences will be the starting point for building credentials necessary for career success. At a minimum, this should include:

- choosing a major in an area conducive to the needs of nonprofit organizations
- developing strong communication skills (both oral and written)
- taking courses, when available, that relate specifically to future work competencies
- achieving experiences through extracurricular activities, summer employment, or other activities that build skills related to the job demands of fund-raising careers
- developing a track record of academic success and personal development that will look attractive to potential employers

INTERNSHIPS

One way to gain valuable experience while still a student is to serve as an intern. Internships in nonprofit organizations can provide valuable opportunities to supplement learning that takes place in the classroom, especially if that experience includes assisting in planning or implementing fund-raising projects.

By serving as an intern, you gain an inside look at what it's like to work in fund-raising or a related field. You also make contacts that can prove valuable in the future for job reference and other purposes. Such experiences could just lead to future employment with the organization where you serve as an intern.

In some cases, students serve as interns while still completing an undergraduate degree. In others, they pursue internships while working on a master's or other graduate degree.

Here are some typical duties for interns in positions related to fund-raising:

- conducting research on prospective donors
- assembling or updating mailing lists
- assisting in planning or coordinating special events
- researching and writing grant proposals
- writing news releases and promotional materials
- helping plan direct mail campaigns
- assisting in clerical tasks and office organization
- helping evaluate the effectiveness of fund-raising projects

A good example is the Summer Internship Program offered by the American Cancer Society. In this program, interns help establish networks in communities to provide outreach programs, identify volunteers within the community to deliver cancer control programs, and increase fund-raising efforts. Students gain real-life experience that can be of use later when seeking permanent positions.

The program is held for eight weeks during the summer and offers opportunities in various locations throughout the country. Students receive a paid stipend that increases in repeat years. To qualify, students must be full-time undergraduates in good academic standing who are completing the freshman year or above. Candidates must earn a B average (cumulative 3.0 on a 4.0-grade scale) and maintain a cumulative B average each year in order to continue in the program. In addition, potential interns must demonstrate a relationship between their projected major field of study and the work of the American Cancer Society. A serious interest in pursuing a career in the nonprofit sector also must be demonstrated.

To be considered for selection, candidates must submit a one-page essay; a resume of educational and job history, honors, awards, and similar information; an official transcript; and two letters of recommendation from advisors or instructors.

For more information contact:

Summer Internship Program
  American Cancer Society
  1599 Clifton Road
  Atlanta, GA 30329

Other organizations offer similar internship opportunities. In addition, those without formal internship programs may be willing to provide a similar experience if approached by a serious student.

SPECIALIZED FUND-RAISING TRAINING PROGRAMS

In addition to the undergraduate college curriculum, a number of other educational options are available to help prepare for a fund-raising career or to advance professionally once employed in the field. These include programs and activities offered by colleges and universities, professional associations, and others.

Even though many of these opportunities are designed for persons already working in the field who want to expand their knowledge and skills, a number are also open to students who would like to strengthen their employment possibilities in nonprofit organizations. Some also provide graduate degree possibilities that may be completed after a bachelor's degree is obtained. Following is an overview of some of these specialized training programs.

Indiana University Center on Philanthropy

The Indiana University Center on Philanthropy offers a number of courses addressing key skills needed in fund-raising and related areas. Many courses may be taken individually as professional development opportunities or to build skills in specific areas related to fund-raising. A typical course may be completed over a three-to-five-day period. Course topics include:

Fund-Raising for Small Nonprofits
Principles and Techniques of Fund-Raising
Planned Giving: Getting the Proper Start
Preparing Successful Grant Proposals
Building the Annual Fund
Managing the Capital Campaign
Developing Leadership for Major Gifts
Enhancing Donor Relations

These courses are offered on a noncredit (CEU or continuing education unit) basis, but some also can form the basis for college credit if additional work is completed. Completion of a specified selection of required courses can lead to a Certificate in Fund-Raising Management.

Indiana University also offers a Master of Public Affairs in Nonprofit Management that can provide a solid background for a career in fund-raising or related areas. Designed for those employed in nonprofit agencies or those who want to enter the field, this program emphasizes the art and craft of developing, managing, and distributing resources for the common good. The program is a collaborative effort of the Indiana University Center on Philanthropy and the university's School of Public and Environmental Affairs.

Students enrolled in this program complete twenty-one credit hours of core courses in public affairs and management. They also complete eighteen credit hours of liberal arts and concentration courses covering various aspects of the nonprofit sector, and an additional nine credit hours of electives or mid-career courses. A total of forty-eight credit hours is needed to complete this program.

Courses in the program (some of which are required and some which are elective) include the following:

Professional Development Practicum: Information Technology
Public Management in the 21st Century
Professional Development Practicum: Writing and Presentation
Professional Development Practicum: Teamwork and
    Integrated Policy Project
Statistical Analysis for Effective Decisionmaking
Public Management Economics
Law and Public Affairs
Public Finance and Budgeting
Capstone in Public and Environmental Affairs
The Nonprofit and Voluntary Sector
Nonprofit Management
The Nonprofit Economy and Public Policy
History of Philanthropy in the West
Ethics and Values of Philanthropy
Civil Society and Public Policy in the U.S.
Civil Society in Comparative Perspective
Legal Aspects of Philanthropy
Human Resource Management in Nonprofit Organizations

Financial Management for Nonprofit Organizations
Fund Development for Nonprofit Organizations
Proposal Development and Grant Administration
Strategic Planning for Public and Nonprofit Organizations
Public Management Information Systems
Management Science for Public Affairs
Benefit–Cost Analysis of Public and Environmental Policies
Public Program Evaluation
Executive Leadership
Individual and Group Behavior

Program admission requirements include a bachelor's degree from an accredited college or university, specified grades and scores on the Graduate Record Examination or comparable exam, and three letters of recommendation. Students who do not meet all these requirements may be admitted on a provisional basis.

For more information contact program officials at:

Indiana University Center on Philanthropy
    Philanthropic Studies Program
    550 West North Street, Suite 301
    Indianapolis, IN 46202-3162

Mandel Center

Another program that includes instruction related to fund-raising is the Master of Nonprofit Organizations (MNO) degree program offered by the Mandel Center of Case Western Reserve University in Cleveland, Ohio, which also offers a Certificate in Nonprofit Management (CNM).

The MNO program is designed for managers and leaders in various nonprofit organizations. Course work in this curriculum focuses on concerns of nonprofit organizations in areas including resource development and fund-raising, among other topics.

The Certificate in Nonprofit Management (CNM) is a nondegree program designed primarily for experienced professionals in nonprofit positions. It serves those who do not necessarily seek an advanced degree, but desire credentials in the specific areas addressed by the program. It is offered through a distance-learning format involving self-paced learning with two twelve-day residencies.

Courses in these programs include the following:

Introduction to the Nonprofit Sector
Ethics, Professionalism, and Leadership
Quantitative Methods for Nonprofit Organizations
Economics for Nonprofit Organizations
Organizations and Management
Financial Accounting and Reporting
Financial Management
Management of Human Resources
Marketing Management
Management of Information Systems
Law of Nonprofit Organizations
Practica
Volunteer Management
Introduction to Arts Management
Trusteeship: Governance of Nonprofit Organizations
Attracting Government, Foundation, and Corporate Support
Conducting Annual, Federated, and Membership Campaigns
Major Gift, Planned Giving, and Capital Campaign Fund-Raising

For more information about these or related courses and programs, contact:

Case Western Reserve University
   The Mandel Center
   10900 Euclid Avenue
   Cleveland, OH 44106

Seton Hall University

Seton Hall University in South Orange, New Jersey, offers a certificate in Nonprofit Organization Management that includes instruction in the fund-raising process. The overall purpose of the program is assisting leaders and administrators of nonprofit organizations in developing or updating management skills.

This fifteen-credit certificate program is offered in conjunction with a master's degree program in public administration, and the credits earned can be applied toward that degree. Available courses include:

Foundations of the Nonprofit Sector
Leadership and Management in Nonprofit Organizations
Public Policy Process, Analysis, and Evaluation
Resource Development
Management of Fiscal Resources
Nonprofit Information Management Systems
Legal Issues in Nonprofit Agencies
Collaborations
Grantsmanship
Human Resource and Volunteer Management
Outcomes Evaluation
Privatization

For information contact:

Seton Hall University
Nonprofit Organization Management Program
400 South Orange Avenue
South Orange, NJ 07079

California State University, Long Beach

Another program of interest is the certificate program in Nonprofit and Public Organization Marketing and Fundraising offered by California State University at Long Beach. The program consists of six modules, with each module made up of six class. Examples of modules include:

Annual Giving, Membership Clubs, and Corporate Giving. Topics include the six-step process in successful membership development, constructing effective solicitation letters, and maximizing board member productivity.

Marketing and Communication. Topics include marketing principles and how they enhance fund-raising and development, how to develop a written marketing plan, and cause-related marketing techniques.

Special Event Marketing. Topics include creating an effective event time line, attracting corporate sponsors to your event, working with volunteers effectively, and attracting celebrities to your event.

Major Gifts and Capital Campaigns. Major topics are effective solicitation techniques and strategies, major donor cultivation techniques, and the six essential steps of a capital campaign.

Corporate and Foundation Grant Solicitation. Topics include writing successful grant proposals, how to research and find grant sources, and writing effective case statements.

Planned Giving Fundamentals. Topics address planned giving, including donor tax benefits and implications; benefits of charitable remainder trusts, charitable gift annuities, and charitable lead trusts; and basics of administering a planned giving program.

For more information contact:

American Institute for Philanthropic Studies
    California State University, Long Beach
    University College and Extension Services
    6300 State University Drive, Suite 104
    Long Beach, CA 90815

Learning Institute for Nonprofit Organizations

The Learning Institute for Nonprofit Organizations is a program resulting from collaboration between the Society for Nonprofit Organizations and the University of Wisconsin-Extension. Originally consisting of instructional programs broadcast live via video satellite, the format has been redesigned for other types of formats such as videotape learning kits and web-based video materials.

Participants in these training programs may take advantage of live programming via satellite, or they may work on a self-paced basis.

Examples of training topics include:

Strategic Planning: Charting Your Course for Success
Resource Development: Involvement and Investment
Board Governance: Building Passion for Mission
Marketing: Connecting with Your Clients and Community
Mission-Based Management: Getting More Mission for Your
    Money
Social Entrepreneurship: Financially Empowering Your Organi-
    zation
Volunteer Management: Attracting and Keeping the Best
Strategic Alliances: Enhancing Your Effectiveness

For more details contact:

Learning Institute Programs
    The Society for Nonprofit Organizations
    6314 Odana Road, Suite 1
    Madison, WI 53719

National Society of Fund Raising
Executives Training Programs

A major provider of educational opportunities in fund-raising is the National Society of Fund Raising Executives (NSFRE) based in Alexandria, Virignia (see Chapter 8 for more details about this organization, including contact information). Activities include:

- NSFRE's International Conference on Fund-Raising, offering more than 150 educational sessions annually.
- The organization's First Course in Fund-Raising, targeted to newcomers in development.
- The Survey Course in Fund-Raising, designed for those who have worked in fund-raising for five years.
- The Executive Leadership Institute, offered to the senior executive with at least seven years' experience as a professional fund-raiser.
- NSFRE's Executive Management Institute, also designed for highly experienced professionals.

In addition, local NSFRE chapters often offer their own educational programs, workshops, and seminars. Some chapters collaborate with a nearby college or university to offer courses in fund-raising.

For more information contact a local NSFRE chapter or contact the national offices at the address provided in Chapter 8.

The Grantsmanship Center

A great source of training in the area of grant development is the Grantsmanship Center. Since 1972 this organization has offered grantsmanship training and publications, primarily serving non-profit organizations and government agencies.

Every year the center sponors about two hundred workshops in grantsmanship, proposal writing, and fund-raising. Many of them are hosted by local agencies. The center publishes a magazine and a guide to proposal writing, and also collects actual grant proposals that have been funded and makes them available on CD-ROM.

For more information, contact the center at:

The Grantsmanship Center
1125 West Sixth Street, Fifth Floor
P.O. Box 17220
Los Angeles, CA 90017

Madison Institute

For those employed or interested in fund-raising within the health care field, the annual Madison Institute, sponsored by the Association for Healthcare Philanthropy in cooperation with the University of Wisconsin's Graduate School of Business, is a weeklong educational and networking opportunity held during the summer. Typical tracks from which participants choose include the fundamentals of resource development, annual giving, major gifts and capital campaigns, planned giving, and fund-raising management.

The AHP also offers a series of self-study guides designed to allow resource development professionals to improve fund-raising skills while learning at their own pace. More than thirty guides are available, including several that have been translated into French.

Available guides include:

Introduction to Health Care Resource Development (U.S. version)
Introduction to Health Care Resource Development (Canadian version)
Elements of Fund-Raising
Professional Ethics
The Psychology of Giving

Prospect and Donor Cultivation
Planning, Managing, and Evaluating Special Events
Corporate Solicitation
Direct Mail Solicitation
Major Gift Cultivation and Solicitation
Board and Family Solicitation
Support Groups and Community Organization
Patient Solicitation
Person-to-Person Solicitation
Medical Staff Solicitation
Memorial and Tribute Gift Solicitation
Foundation Grantsmanship and Proposal Writing
Researching Grant Opportunities
Use of the Telephone in Resource Development
Introduction to Annual Giving
Setting up the Annual Giving Program
Managing and Evaluating the Annual Giving Program
Introduction to Planned Giving
Setting up the Planned Giving Program
Managing and Evaluating the Planned Giving Program
Understanding the Planned Giving Instruments (U.S. version)
Understanding the Planned Giving Instruments (Canadian version)
Introduction to the Capital Campaign
Setting up the Capital Campaign
Managing and Evaluating the Capital Campaign
Introduction to Public Relations
Managing and Evaluating the Public Relations Program
Introduction to Marketing
Marketing for Health Care Resource Development
Writing the Case Statement
Fund-Raising Copy
Publication Design and Production
Public Speaking

For more information contact:

Association for Healthcare Philanthropy
    313 Park Avenue, Suite 400
    Falls Church, VA 22046

Center for the Study of Philanthropy

The programs sponsored by the Center for the Study of Philanthropy of the City University of New York cover several areas related to fund-raising. This center focuses its programs in four major areas: women and philanthropy, multiculturalism, international and comparative research, and the City of New York. It sponsors an International Fellows Program, employs more than thirty graduate assistants working on various aspects of its program, and sponsors fellowships and other award programs for talented students to encourage the study of philanthropy.

The center also sponsors publications including special issues of the *Nonprofit and Voluntary Sector Quarterly* and other publications on giving, voluntarism, and so forth.

The center has developed a variety of courses for the undergraduate and graduate curriculum on philanthropic topics and hosts conferences and seminars on related subjects.

For more information contact the center at:

Center for the Study of Philanthropy
    365 Fifth Avenue, 5th Floor
    New York, NY 10016–4309

Vanderbilt University

Peabody College of Vanderbilt University offers graduate courses in Institutional Advancement. Students who pursue master's or doctoral degrees in higher education may pursue a specialty in Institutional Advancement, which includes courses on fund-raising and related topics within the college and university setting.

For more information contact:

Peabody College
  Vanderbilt University
  Nashville, TN 37203

CHAPTER 8

PROFESSIONAL ASSOCIATIONS AND RESOURCES

It has been said that nobody operates in a vacuum. This is certainly true in the fund-raising community, where working with other people is a key element of career success. Professionals in this field, as well as graduate students and others aspiring to fund-raising careers, can benefit greatly from interacting with others who face similar challenges. That is the main premise behind professional associations, where people who work in different organizations are linked together by common interests.

Typically a professional association consists of voluntary members—sometimes numbering in the thousands in the case of larger groups—who join together to share information, pool resources, or otherwise achieve common goals. Officers are usually elected from the membership, with a core staff of paid managers and support personnel coordinating the association's activities. Their combined efforts provide services to members to help them perform their jobs more effectively.

ADVANTAGES OF PROFESSIONAL ASSOCIATIONS

Why participate in professional associations? The reasons vary, but in general most participants benefit in some or all of the following ways:

96

- networking with colleagues who face similar challenges in carrying out their jobs
- learning from senior members or those with expertise in specific areas of interest
- participating in conferences sponsored by the organization
- keeping up with new developments through newsletters, magazines, websites, or other means of communication
- gaining "strength in numbers" where the association's combined membership may use its clout to influence legislation, gain group rates for personal needs such as life insurance, or achieve other goals
- using the stature of the association to add credibility to the fund-raising efforts of local organizations
- emphasizing and promoting ethical practices in fund-raising
- gaining new knowledge though formal professional development activities as well as informal communications
- identifying and pursuing job openings

OVERVIEW OF ASSOCIATIONS AND RESOURCES

Following is an overview of a number of associations serving the nonprofit sector in general and those that work in fund-raising specifically, along with profiles of a few other helpful resources.

The Foundation Center

A highly respected organization providing helpful resources to fund-raising professionals is the Foundation Center, headquartered in New York City. For more than forty years, the center has promoted public understanding of the foundation field. Its activities include collecting, organizing, analyzing, and disseminating information on foundations, corporate giving, and related matters.

An especially popular service among grant seekers is the information made available at Foundation Center libraries New York City, Washington, DC, Atlanta, Cleveland, and San Francisco. These libraries provide a wide range of materials on fund-raising and philanthropy and are open to the public at no cost. Reference materials include Internal Revenue Service returns filed annually by more than forty thousand U.S. private foundations, foundation annual reports, corporate giving reports, newsletters, directories, books, and periodicals. A number of directories and guides are also available for purchase, and the center provides literature online through its website.

For more information contact the center at:

The Foundation Center
79 Fifth Avenue
New York, NY 10003–3076

Addresses of other Foundation Center libraries are:

Washington, DC

1001 Connecticut Avenue NW, Suite 938
Washington, DC 20036

Atlanta

50 Hurt Plaza, Suite 150
Atlanta, GA 30303-2914

Cleveland

1422 Euclid Avenue, Suite 1356
Cleveland, OH 44115-2001

San Francisco

312 Sutter Street, Suite 606
San Francisco, CA 94108-4314

Council on Foundations

Another helpful organization is the Council on Foundations, based in Washington, DC. This group has approximately eighteen hundred member organizations including community foundations, corporate foundations, family foundations, private operating foundations, private independent foundations, and other organizations. The council provides programs for staff, trustees, and board members of foundations. Although the emphasis is on grant making activities rather than fund-raising, the council can be a useful resource in helping fund-raising professionals understand and stay current with issues facing foundations.

For more information contact:

Council on Foundations
 1828 L Street, NW
 Washington, DC 20036

National Society of Fund Raising Executives

The National Society of Fund Raising Executives (NSFRE) is a good source of information about the fund-raising profession and support for those involved. This association has more than twenty-thousand members in chapters located throughout the United States and Canada. Members hold a wide range of jobs in non-profit and charitable organizations.

Major purposes of this association include:

- promoting high standards of professional practice
- promoting ethical principles and standards
- protecting the rights and interests of donors
- offering a professional certification process
- providing educational programs about fund-raising, publications for members, and information about philanthropy

- encouraging research on fund-raising and philanthropy
- supporting legislation and regulations to encourage ethical fund-raising and philanthropic giving

Professional development opportunities provided by NSFRE are quite diverse. They include an annual International Conference on Fund-Raising, other conferences, and special offerings such as the First Course in Fund-Raising (a two-day seminar for new professionals), the Survey Course on Fund-Raising, an Executive Leadership Institute, and an Executive Management Institute.

In addition, the association's Fund-Raising Resource Center maintains a large collection of books, periodicals, and other informational materials about fund-raising and the nonprofit world.

Publications include *Advancing Philanthropy,* a quarterly magazine about the fund-raising profession; *NSFRE News,* a newsletter; and *Profile,* a research-based monograph.

Of special interest to those wishing to build professional credentials is the association's certification program. This program demonstrates to employers, donors, and others that the professional has attained a significant level of experience and knowledge. This Certified Fund-Raising Executive (CFRE) designation may be earned by fund-raising professionals with at least five years of experience. To earn it, they must successfully complete an application and examination process.

An Advanced Certified Fund-Raising Executive (ACFRE) designation process is also offered by the association. It is available to those with at least ten years of professional experience.

Another helpful service is the sharing of information about job openings. The NSFRE's *Employment Opportunities* newsletter, which is published monthly, provides job listings of possible interest to members.

For more information about these and other services, contact:

National Society of Fund Raising Executives
  1101 King Street, Suite 700
  Alexandria, VA 22314-2967

Canadian Centre for Philanthropy

The Canadian Centre for Philanthropy is an organization dedicated to advancing the interests of the charitable sector for the benefit of Canadian communities. This association serves charitable organizations as well as the corporations and foundations that support them.

The centre provides a number of benefits to members. These include:

- information about Canada's charitable sector such as "issue alerts" dealing with important public policy issues
- an annual symposium that covers important issues
- publications including the *Centre News* newsletter; a newspaper, *Front & Centre;* and research bulletins and other studies covering trends in donations, fund-raising methods, funding sources, and other topics related to fund-raising and philanthropy
- an "Ethical Fund-Raising and Financial Accountability Code" that promotes ethical standards and accountability

For more information contact the centre at:

Canadian Centre for Philanthropy
  425 University Avenue, 7th Floor
  Toronto, ON Canada M5G 1T6

Council for Advancement and Support of Education

The Council for Advancement and Support of Education (CASE) supports advancement in the educational community. It provides information and training in areas such as alumni relations, communications, government relations, and fund-raising.

Publications provided to members include *Currents,* a magazine published ten times a year; the *CASE Membership Directory; Flash Points,* an issues management bulletin; and "issues papers" on various topics of interest. Online discussion groups also serve advancement officers at two-year colleges, senior members of the advancement profession, and alumni relations professionals at colleges, universities, and independent schools. The association provides books, bibliographies, videos, and research guidelines through its information center.

CASE sponsors more that 140 different types of conferences yearly. These range from one-day regional workshops to week-long comprehensive summer institutes. While these are open to nonmembers, members receive substantial discounts on registration fees.

Another helpful service is the National Clearinghouse for Matching Gift Information. This clearinghouse encourages and monitors the practice in which corporations and foundations match gifts that their employees make to charitable organizations and provides information to members to assist in this process.

The council also supports ethical standards and sponsors recognition programs. For more information contact:

Council for Advancement and Support of Education
    11 Dupont Circle, Suite 400
    Washington, DC 20036

American Association of Fund-Raising Counsel

The American Association of Fund-Raising Counsel (AAFRC) is a trade association of consulting firms that work within the fund-raising and philanthropic community. This organization, which has been in existence since 1935, works to advance philanthropy and promote ethical approaches to fund-raising.

Among other services, the organization provides contact information for member consulting firms. This can be of potential use to those interested in the possibility of arranging internships with consulting firms, as well as those with appropriate credentials who are seeking employment.

For more information contact:

American Association of Fund-Raising Counsel
   25 West 43rd Street
   New York, NY 10036

Association for Healthcare Philanthropy

The Association for Healthcare Philanthropy serves fund-raising professionals who work in health care organizations in a number of ways. Among its most valuable services are a number of publications, including:

AHP Connect. Highlights the association's members, events, and activities while providing general information on fund-raising matters in health care. A "Positions Available" section lists job openings.

AHP Journal. Contains articles on health care resource development.

A membership directory and buyers' guide.

The AHP Foundation's report on giving in the United States and Canada. Provides detailed information on giving to health care institutions.

Compensation reports.

Topical reports on issues related to health care philanthropy.

AHP Development Primer Manual. Provides a comprehensive outline of fund-raising basics.

For more information contact:

Association for Healthcare Philanthropy
313 Park Avenue, Suite 400
Falls Church, VA 22046

American Prospect Research Association

This association supports the work of advancement researchers and related professionals working within the nonprofit community. Its goals include:

- promoting professional growth and advancement
- advocating high standards of performance and ethical behavior
- facilitating interaction among research, development, and information professionals and their representative organizations
- advancing the role of research in the development field

Membership benefits include:

- two quarterly publications, the *Bulletin* and *Connections,* and a resource/membership directory
- an annual conference as well as regional conferences sponsored by more than twenty-five chapters of the association
- a "job bank" that maintains information on job openings
- an awards program

For more details contact:

American Prospect Research Association
414 Plaza Drive
Westmont, IL 60559

Council for Resource Development

The Council for Resource Development (CRD) is an affiliate of the American Association of Community Colleges. This organization includes more than one thousand people, representing over eight hundred two-year colleges in the United States and Canada.

Benefits to members include substantial networking opportunities as well as educational and professional development opportunities. These include:

1. An annual three-day conference in Washington, DC that offers presentations on public and private sector fund-raising and project management.
2. Regional conferences held annually in each of the ten regions of the United States and Canada.
3. A Resource Development Specialist Training Program, which can be especially helpful to newcomers in the field. This two-week intensive program provides an in-depth study of fund-raising and project management. The initial week is held on a model two-year college campus, while the second week of study takes place in Washington, DC.
4. A Summer Symposium on Emerging Issues, which provides professional development opportunities for experienced advancement officers.

Publications include an *Annual Membership Directory and Resource Guide;* a newsletter, *Dispatch,* published three times a year; an annual *Federal Funding to Two-Year Colleges Report;* a corporate funding brochure; and various resource papers. In addition, *The Best of CRD* is a videotape featuring the basics of proposal writing and strategies for developing successful proposals.

For more information contact:

Council for Resource Development
    One Dupont Circle NW, Suite 410
    Washington, DC 20036

Society for Nonprofit Organizations

This organization serves as a resource for those who lead or help nonprofit organizations all around the world. Major activities of the society include:

- publishing a bimonthly magazine on nonprofit issues
- publishing a monthly report on funding opportunities for nonprofit organizations
- providing books, audiotapes, and videotapes geared specifically to nonprofits
- providing training opportunities

For more details contact:

The Society for Nonprofit Organizations
6314 Odana Road, Suite 1
Madison, WI 53719

National Committee on Planned Giving

The National Committee on Planned Giving is a professional association for those whose work includes developing, marketing, or administering charitable planned gifts. Members include fundraisers for nonprofit organizations as well as consultants and donor advisors employed by for-profit businesses.

Formed in 1988, the committee facilitates, coordinates, and encourages the education and training of the planned giving community; and facilitates effective communication among professionals in the community.

The committee publishes the *Journal of Gift Planning,* a quarterly publication, as well as other publications. It promotes legislation favorable to the planned giving community, holds conferences for members, and sponsors research projects. It also offers a web-based job-posting service.

For more information contact:

National Committee on Planned Giving
  233 McCrea Street, Suite 400
  Indianapolis, IN 46225

Canadian Association of Gift Planners

The Canadian Association of Gift Planners supports philanthropy by fostering the development and growth of gift planning. Serving as an advocate of charitable giving, the association has the following purposes:

- creating awareness
- providing education
- bringing together professionals from various disciplines to ensure that the gift planning process achieves a fair and proper balance between the interests of donors and those of charitable organizations
- promoting standards of professional and ethical practice

Members of the association include persons responsible for gift planning programs of registered charitable organizations or foundations, fund-raising consultants, attorneys, accountants, financial planners, trust officers, and other professionals.

Functioning as a national organization, the association has roundtables operating in every region and most major cities in Canada.

For more information contact:

Canadian Association of Gift Planners
P.O. Box 4084
Edmonton, AL Canada T6E 4S8

American College of Trust and Estate Counsel

Although it serves a membership of attorneys rather than those who work strictly as advancement professionals, the American College of Trust and Estate Counsel is a professional association worth noting due to the publications and services it provides, especially for those interested in working in the planned giving area. The membership consists of approximately twenty-seven hundred lawyers from across the United States.

Prospective members cannot apply for membership but instead are invited to participate. Selections are based on professional reputation, ability in the fields of trusts and estates, and achievement of substantial contributions such as lecturing, writing, teaching, and bar activities.

Purposes of the American College of Trust and Estate Counsel are:

1. To maintain an international association of lawyers skilled and experienced in the preparation of wills and trusts, estate planning, probate procedure, and administration of trusts and estates of decedents, minors, and incompetents;

2. To improve and reform probate, trust and tax laws, procedures, and professional responsibility;

3. To bring together qualified lawyers whose character and ability contribute to the achievement of the purposes of the college; and

4. To cooperate with bar associations and other organizations with similar purposes.

Additional information about this association is available by contacting:

American College of Trust and Estate Counsel (ACTEC)
   3415 South Sepulveda Boulevard, Suite 330
   Los Angeles, CA 90034

Society of Research Administrators

The Society of Research Administrators has existed since 1967 to advance the profession and improve the efficiency and effectiveness of research administration. The association has more than twenty-eight hundred members from the United States, Canada, and other nations. It serves as a professional society for research administrators in a variety of settings.

Among its services to members are:

- an extensive network of divisions, sections, chapters, and interest groups
- a variety of seminars, meetings, and workshops offered at the local, regional, national, and international levels
- publications including the *SRA Journal* and the *SRA News*
- partnerships and other programs to promote diversity
- a mentoring program
- communication services including information on job openings
- recognition programs

In addition to state and local chapters, the society consists of the following sections:

Southern Section
Midwest Section
Northeast Section

Western Section
Canadian Section

More information is available from:

Society of Research Administrators
1200 19th Street NW, Suite 300
Washington, DC 20036

Canadian Marketing Association

The Canadian Marketing Association represents information-based marketers not only in the business sector, but also those working in charitable organizations who perform similar work. Members of the association include more than 750 organizations and 3,000 individual members in councils, committees, and regional chapters.

Established in 1967, the group has an elected board of directors nominated from the association membership, and it is managed by a full-time professional staff.

The association focuses on successful self-regulation and offers a strict code of ethics and a privacy code. It publishes *The Communicator,* a quarterly newsletter, and provides other publications.

For more information contact:

Canadian Marketing Association
1 Concord Gate
Don Mills, ON Canada M3C 3N6

National Council for Marketing and Public Relations

The National Council for Marketing and Public Relations (NCMPR) serves individuals working in marketing, communications, and public relations at two-year colleges, many of whom serve as part of a development or advancement office. NCMPR provides professional development opportunities, recognizes professional excellence, and serves as an advocate for the field.

The organization is an affiliate council of the American Association of Community Colleges and has more than fourteen hundred members in the United States, Canada, and elsewhere. It sponsors conferences, provides publications, and offers extensive networking and professional recognition opportunities.

More information is available by contacting:

National Council for Marketing and Public Relations
    4602 West 21st Street Circle
    Greeley, CO 80634

National Council of Nonprofit Associations

The National Council of Nonprofit Associations (NCNA) is a network of more than forty state and regional associations. The collective membership of these groups is more than twenty thousand community nonprofit organizations.

The council is an advocate for support for the nonprofit sector. Types of organizations it serves include social, service, education, health, and cultural organizations.

For more information contact:

National Council of Nonprofit Associations
    1900 L Street NW
    Washington, DC 20036

National Federation of Nonprofits

This organization addresses issues such as state and federal regulation, charity "watchdog" activities, postal regulations and practices, and other issues. Founded in 1982 as the Nonprofit Mailers Federation, the organization changed it name in 1993 to reflect the broadening variety of topics it covers ranging from nonprofit accounting to maintaining relations with regulators.

For more information contact:

National Federation of Nonprofits, Inc.
815 15th Street NW, Suite 822
Washington, DC 20005

CHAPTER 9

SALARIES AND BENEFITS

Salaries earned by fund-raising professionals and related employees of nonprofit organizations vary widely. In a small, local organization, salaries may be much lower than those earned by employees performing work of equivalent complexity in a private business. In a university or large national organization, salaries may be quite good, especially for experienced fund-raisers or for those with substantial management responsibilities.

In general, salaries paid by nonprofit employers are not as high as those for comparable positions in private business. Since nonprofit organizations rely on government funding or private donations, they tend to have a different philosophy about salaries, often keeping them from becoming so high that they detract from the organization's public service image. Benefits such as stock options and profit-sharing plans are not available in the nonprofit sector.

Still, salaries can be quite attractive. In addition, many employers offer liberal fringe benefits.

SALARY RANGES

According to Ohio State University, development directors earn salaries ranging from $25,000 to $80,000 yearly. Factors influencing the range include seniority, size and type of employing organization, and variances in the cost of living in different geographical areas.

In a survey conducted by the *Non-Profit Times,* development directors in nonprofit organizations reported an average salary of $46,695 in 1998. In the same survey, planned giving officers reported average salaries of $53,429. The higher salary for this specialized role may be accounted for by the fact that many smaller organizations are unlikely to have the resources to support positions devoted entirely to planned giving, while larger, more affluent employers can support this function. In a larger organization, senior development directors' salaries may be higher than those of planned giving officers.

In another survey published in the *Chronicle of Higher Education,* fund-raising personnel in colleges and universities had median salaries ranging from about $38,500 to $84,000 in 1998–99, depending on the type of institution and the nature of the position held. The highest salaries were earned by chief development officers at doctorate-granting universities (positions such as vice president for development or vice president for advancement), with annual salaries of more than $100,000 not uncommon. Fund-raising personnel at smaller four-year colleges and two-year colleges earned significantly less.

As a group, the top earning positions, listed in descending order, were:

Chief Development Officer
Government Relations Officer
Director of Major Gifts
Director of Planned Giving
Director of Corporate and Foundation Relations
Director of Alumni Affairs
Director of Annual Giving
Coordinator of Resource Development

Following are some examples of salaries paid to those holding fund-raising positions at several types of organizations; they are taken from current announcements for job openings:

Position	Employer	Salary
Director of Development	Public television station, Virginia	$40–50,000
Director of Annual Giving	State-supported college, New York	$50–55,000
Executive Director	Public College Foundation, New York	$50–55,000
Director of Development	Equal rights organization, California	$60–70,000
Director of Development	Conservation organization, Washington, DC	$40–50,000
Campaign Manager	Arts organization, Texas	$20–25,000
Manager, Corporate and Foundation Gifts	Public library, Washington	$47–58,000
Prospect Researcher	Public televison station, Oregon	$28–34,000
Coordinator of Advancement	Public community college, Virginia	$40–50,000
Grants Manager	Private four-year college, New York	$30–35,000

Obviously, those organizations that have a strong funding base are more likely to pay higher salaries. At the same time, employers offering lower salaries may provide a good place to pursue a fund-raising career. There may be less competition for landing a job in the first place, and applicants who are short on experience may be more likely to get a chance to learn on the job.

After gaining work experience at a relatively low paying job, there is always the possibility of seeking another position that offers a more attractive salary. The skills and knowledge gained in the first job can enhance your qualifications and eligibility to be considered for other positions.

Actually, salaries vary not only from one type of fund-raising position to another, but for a variety of reasons. A number of factors can influence levels, including the following:

Educational background. In many cases, fund-raising professionals who have earned advanced degrees earn higher salaries than those with a bachelor's as their highest degree. This is especially common in colleges or other educational organizations, which often have salary schedules in place that include educational level as a major factor in determining salary level.

Skill and experience. Understandably those with extensive experience tend to earn higher salaries. This is true both for long-time employees within a given organization and for those who move from one organization to another. With the former, a pattern of annual salary increases may lead to a progressively higher salary. With the latter, an employer may be willing to pay a higher salary to attract experienced professionals.

Location. Geographical location is a major determinant in establishing salary levels. Those who work in large cities tend to earn more than staff members in more rural areas, and the same is true in areas where the cost of living is higher. For instance, fund-raising professionals working in Los Angeles or Boston tend to earn more than those employed in Jackson, Mississippi, or Missoula, Montana.

Economic conditions. Factors such as inflation and the overall state of the economy affect salary levels. Most full-time employees receive annual raises that take inflation, along with other factors, into account.

Size and type of employer. With so much variety in types and sizes of nonprofit organizations, it is not surprising that they tend to pay employees, including fund-raising professionals, at widely differing levels. The chief development officer in a large private university, for example, will earn significantly more than the holder of a comparable position in a small community college. Similarly, a small local charity will not have the resources to pay salaries as high as those at major national organizations.

Level of responsibility. In general, the greater the level of responsibility, the higher the salary. Senior development officers have a number of responsibilities including not only direct fund-raising, but also management duties. They must hire, supervise, and evaluate other employees; develop plans for fund-raising operations; and perform other duties. At the higher levels, they may serve as a key part of an organization's overall management team.

Correspondingly, those holding entry-level jobs or those at lower organizational levels command lower salaries.

Existing salary. In many cases, job vacancy announcements do not list salaries, but instead use phrases such as the following:

"Please describe salary history."
"Send letter of application with salary requirements."
"Salary is commensurate with education and experience."

Normally this means that your current salary will be taken into account if you are offered a position, with the salary to be offered to be based, at least in part, on your current salary. At the same time, most organizations have ranges within which they operate, and they will not offer a salary beyond a pre-established upper limit. But for an experienced professional, they may offer a salary at the upper range of the normal pay schedule.

Competition for employees. The greater the demand for qualified employees, the higher salaries tend to rise. In recent years the demand for qualified fund-raising professionals has been great as more and more organizations initiate or expand fund-raising programs. This has contributed to an overall increase in salary levels.

Performance-Based Pay

In some cases fund-raisers are paid on the basis of the volume of funds they bring to an organization. This practice is frowned upon by many in the nonprofit community. The National Society of Fund Raising Executives, for example, considers this an unethical practice and urges that it be avoided.

FRINGE BENEFITS

Most employers provide a variety of benefits to employees in addition to salaries. These can be a significant plus, especially in an era when many employers in the for-profit sector are cutting costs by reducing the levels of benefits provided to employees. Many nonprofit employers, on the other hand, see this as an organizational responsibility and a means of attracting employees.

For example, managerial and professional employees at Yale University may earn fringe benefits in the following categories:

medical insurance
dental insurance
life insurance
travel/accident insurance
disability insurance

holidays
sick time
personal time
retirement plans
retiree benefits
tuition assistance
scholarships for children of employees
death benefits

Some benefits are paid in their entirety by the university, while employees contribute toward the others in varying degrees.

Other employers may not have quite this level of variety, but at a minimum they will provide vacation time, holidays, and medical and retirement plans. Some benefits are paid entirely by the employer, while costs of others are shared by employees.

One benefit of particular interest to those just beginning their careers is educational assistance. This may come in several forms, including the following:

- tuition reimbursement, where the employer reimburses you for the cost of college courses you complete successfully
- direct payment of tuition, where the employer makes direct payment to an educational institution on your behalf
- tuition waivers (offered by colleges and universities for their own employees)
- payment of book costs
- unpaid education leave, where you are allowed to take time off to pursue educational objectives but without needing to quit your job
- paid time off to attend classes

Educational benefits such as these can be great career builders. Those who wish to pursue a master's degree, doctorate, or other advanced degree will find them an important factor to take into account when looking at prospective employers.

When examining job offers, fringe benefits should be considered carefully, since some organizations offer more in this area. Benefits can be especially important in meeting the needs of multiperson families.

CHAPTER 10

GETTING STARTED

Just how do you get started in fund-raising? Here are a few final thoughts.

IDENTIFYING JOB OPENINGS

There is no one method for finding jobs in fund-raising. For students, a good place to start is the career services office of your college. If you're in high school, check with the career services office of a local college that also serves potential students or the public at large.

In seeking jobs, consult the classified sections of major newspapers and watch for ads placed by nonprofit organizations. Although newspapers published in smaller cities will include ads for local job openings, you'll need to consult major papers such as the *New York Times* and *Washington Post* for regional or national openings.

Another strategy is to contact organizations directly and request information on job openings and how you might apply. Many nonprofit organizations now include such information online; start by checking out their sites on the World Wide Web.

Perhaps the best sources of job information are publications targeted specifically to those who are already employed in the nonprofit sector or who have other direct ties such as service on boards of directors.

Probably the most comprehensive source of information about the nonprofit world is the *Chronicle of Philanthropy* newspaper, published on a biweekly basis except for the last two weeks in June and the final two weeks of December.

Of special interest to those hoping to break into the fund-raising field are the *Chronicle*'s extensive job listings. A typical issue includes scores of ads for job openings around the United States and sometimes positions in Canada, with each ad including a position description, job requirements, application deadlines, and other details.

The *Chronicle of Philanthropy* also provides a wealth of information about the nonprofit sector through features articles, news updates and regular columns, and departments.

For subscription details or other information, write to:

The Chronicle of Philanthropy
P.O. Box 1989
Marion, OH 43305

A sister publication, the *Chronicle of Higher Education,* provides similar job listings as those found in the *Chronicle of Philanthropy,* but it focuses on colleges and universities instead of the nonprofit world at large. It is an excellent source for such listings and is widely used by colleges and universities as a publication for announcing job vacancies.

Another good source of information is the *Non-Profit Times.* Published eighteen times a year, this newspaper-style publication provides a wealth of useful information on the nonprofit world, including news, special columns and departments, and ads for various resources related to nonprofit management. A calendar of events is included, along with a resource directory providing information on consulting services, equipment, software, and other resources for fund-raising professionals. Of particular interest to those who wish to break into the field is a section called "Employment Marketplace," which lists job openings around the country, including fund-raising positions.

You can find the *Non-Profit Times* in libraries or in offices at nonprofit organizations. For subscription information contact the publication at:

The Non-Profit Times
   240 Cedar Knolls Road, Suite 318
   Cedar Knolls, NJ 07927

Another publication of interest to fund-raising professionals is *Contributions,* a bimonthly newspaper published by Cambridge Fund Raising Associates. Although it does include advertising, listing job openings is not its purpose. Instead, *Contributions* provides information to help fund-raisers and other nonprofit professionals locate helpful resources or simply learn more about effective ways to do their jobs.

Typical subject matters include:

   direct mail
   board development
   the Internet
   funding trends
   annual giving
   planned giving
   marketing
   prospect research
   grant seeking
   special events
   management
   book reviews

Subscription information and other details are available at:

Contributions
P.O. Box 338
Medfield, MA 02052–0338

Another publication that lists job openings in fund-raising is *Community Jobs*. Published in Washington, DC, and appearing ten times yearly, this publication includes a large number of job announcements in every issue. For subscription information, write to:

Community Jobs
1001 Connecticut Avenue NW
Washington, DC 20036

An Internet-based source of job information is:

The Community Career Center Enterprise, Inc.
2160 West Charleston
Las Vegas, NV 89102

BUILDING AN APPROPRIATE BACKGROUND

Before making any type of commitment toward a career in fund-raising, it's a good idea to gain some firsthand information about the field in general and how your own interests, abilities, and overall goals mesh with the realities of such a job. Here are some steps you can take in this direction. You probably would not want to choose all of them, but following one or more of these strategies may prove worthwhile. Consider some of the following steps while you're still a student or before you make the commitment of actually taking a job in fund-raising.

1. Volunteer at a local nonprofit organization. Contact the United Way or agencies it supports and ask if you can help out in some way related to fund-raising. Or, take the same initiative at the development office or advancement office at

a community college, four-year college, or private high school. By volunteering in this way, you can gain a first-hand look at the day-to-day work involved.

2. Arrange to complete an internship at a nonprofit organization with fund-raising tasks as your major contribution (see Chapter 7 for more details on internships). Keep in mind that the duties typically assigned to interns do not include the more advanced work involved in fund-raising, but the process still can give you a good "inside picture" of what working in this field is like.

3. Pursue a part-time job in fund-raising. A part-time or summer job can provide similar benefits to those provided by an internship, with the added plus of making money. The most likely areas for such jobs would be clerical in nature, but as with internships, part-time work can give you a firsthand look at fund-raising. While working in such a job, a good practice is to take extra effort to study the work performed by others and ask questions about how permanent employees feel about their jobs.

4. Take an interest inventory. Guidance counselors, college career services offices, and job search firms often administer exams that are designed to help you make career choices. These "exams" do not have passing or failing scores, but instead provide an analytical look at your interests based on information you provide in answering questions. Consider taking a test or two of this type, and then discuss your results with a counselor.

5. Enroll in seminars or classes related to fund-raising. As noted in Chapter 7, courses or seminars on fund-raising topics can help prepare you for work in the field. They also can provide additional information that will help you assess your interest levels. Taking just one class before committing to a full program is often a good strategy.

6. Read more about fund-raising. Books and articles about fund-raising are also good sources of information. See Appendix A for some suggested further reading.

FURTHER ENHANCING EMPLOYMENT POTENTIAL

As previously discussed, job openings in the fund-raising area have varying requirements. Some positions require years of specific job experience and would not be a realistic job possibility for a recent college graduate or other newcomer (although they can become a goal for the future). Others are designed as entry-level positions and could be a great way to get started.

In any case, employers routinely consider four basic factors in hiring new staff to work in fund-raising:

1. education
2. experience
3. job-related skills
4. potential

An ideal job candidate will demonstrate strength in all four areas. Of course, any one prospective employee will not demonstrate equal strength in all areas, and few recent college graduates could be expected to have attained extensive job experience. But to enhance your own job prospects, do everything possible to demonstrate a positive record in all four areas. Here are some tips to increase your odds of success in each area.

Education. Much attention is given to the choice of a major, but don't overlook the potential offered by individual courses. If you take a course in public relations, for example, that can be a good selling point later. The same is true for a course in persuasive writing or grant writing.

You may have to look carefully at other disciplines to identify such courses. A course in grant writing, for example, may be found in your college's social work program or in a public administration curriculum. But even if you are not a social work or public administration major, perhaps you can take it as an elective course. Or, you can take it as a summer course or distance learning course offered by another school.

Remember, completing an entire degree may earn only a few lines on your resume. The ability to list individual courses, seminars, or other learning experiences on a resume or job application can be a real plus in the job search.

Experience. As noted earlier, a variety of options exists for gaining work experience. Summer jobs, part-time jobs, internships, and volunteer work all can provide valuable work experience. This is useful not only in developing appropriate knowledge, but also for the pragmatic need to cite it when applying for job openings.

A key in this process is relating job or volunteer experiences with the expectations of those who work in fund-raising. Of course, any directly related experience should be emphasized, but you can also draw parallels to work experiences that are somewhat similar to fund-raising responsibilities.

For example, if you work in sales, customer service, or similar functions, you could cite that experience as potentially useful in helping you perform fund-raising tasks in a nonprofit organization. The same is true of any work experience involving writing, public relations, or other areas.

Job-related skills. If you do not yet have significant work experience, it may be hard to demonstrate that you possess specific job-related skills that are appropriate for fund-raising positions. But even here, your success as a student shows that you have developed some important skills, and job or volunteer experience can be used to enhance such capabilities.

For instance, any writing skills you can demonstrate will be to your advantage. If you have written articles for a school newspaper, designed ads for a marketing class, or contributed to a church newsletter, you can use that experience as evidence of writing capability.

The same is true if you have taken speech classes or other communications classes, acquired computing skills, or developed other skills that might be applied in the nonprofit setting.

Potential. As noted previously, a successful work experience—especially in a related area—can go a long way. In addition, potential can be evidenced by factors such as:

- good grades
- positive recommendations from teachers or professors
- awards demonstrating specific skills (academic awards, winning entries in speech contests or essay contests, etc.)
- leadership positions
- previous success at volunteer fund-raising
- written or visual evidence of skills mastered (for example, samples of materials you've written, a web page you've developed, etc.)
- traits that demonstrate intelligence such as a strong vocabulary, a good command of grammar and usage, and well-developed conversation skills
- poise and personality as demonstrated in job interviews or social interaction

If you have strengths in any of these areas, take advantage of them. In areas with weaknesses, work on making improvements. With the right combination of education, experience, skills, and potential, you can position yourself to take advantage of position openings when they become available.

The bottom line? Getting started in fund-raising is not all that different from starting out in other fields. Just keep in mind that you will need to acquire some specialized job skills, do what it takes to develop them, and go from there! With a positive attitude and a willingness to work hard, you can contribute to a key component of the nonprofit world: the fund-raising function that helps organizations meet their goals.

APPENDIX A

FURTHER READING

Anderson, Albert. *Ethics for Fundraisers.* Bloomington, IN: Indiana University Press, 1996.

Blum, Laurie. *The Complete Guide to Getting a Grant.* New York: John Wiley and Sons, 1996.

Catalog of Federal Domestic Assistance. Superintendent of Documents, U.S. Government Printing Office, 1999.

Durorio, Margaret and Eugene Tempel. *Fund Raisers: Their Careers, Stories, Concerns and Accomplishments.* San Francisco: Jossey-Bass, 1996.

Geever, Jane and Patricia McNeill. *The Guide to Proposal Writing.* New York: Foundation Center, 1997.

Golden, Susan and Alan Shrader. *Secrets of Successful Grantsmanship.* San Francisco: Jossey-Bass, 1997.

Greenfield, James. *Fund-Raising Fundamentals: A Guide to Annual Giving for Professionals & Volunteers.* New York: John Wiley and Sons, 1994.

Henley, Michael and Diane Hodiak. *Fund Raising in the One-Person Shop: Achieving Success with Limited Resources.* Minneapolis: Development Resource Center, 1998.

Hoffman, Don and others. *Winning Strategies for Developing Grant Proposals.* Washington, DC: Thompson Publishing Group, 1999.

Johnston, Michael. *The Fund Raiser's Guide to the Internet.* New York: John Wiley & Sons, 1996.

Keegan, P. Burke. *Fundraising for Non-Profits.* New York: HarperCollins, 1994.

Lauber, Daniel. *Non-Profits and Education Job Finder: 1997–2000.* Planning Communications, 1997.

Mathis, Emily and John Doody. *Grant Proposals: A Primer for Writers.* Washington, DC: National Catholic Education, 1994.

Morris, James. *Grant Seekers Guide.* Wakefield, RI: Moyer Bell, 1998.

Paradis, Adrian. *Opportunities in Nonprofit Organization Careers.* Lincolnwood, IL: VGM Career Books, 1994.

Poderis, Tony. *It's a Great Day to Fund Raise!* Willoughby Hills, OH: FundAmerica Press, 1997.

Weinstein, Stanley. *The Complete Guide to Fund-Raising Management.* New York: John Wiley and Sons, 1996.

White, Douglas. *The Art of Planned Giving.* New York: John Wiley and Sons, 1998.

Worth, Michael, editor. *Educational Fund Raising: Principles and Practice.* Phoenix, AZ: American Council on Education-Oryx Press, 1996.

TIPS ON PROPOSAL PREPARATION

As noted earlier, writing grant proposals is an important task completed by many fund-raising professionals. This process requires an understanding of the basic elements of a proposal and how to develop them in a manner resulting in an application that will be competitive with others submitted to the same agency or funding organization.

Following is an overview of key aspects involved in developing and writing grant proposals. This overview is adapted from material developed by the federal government's General Services Administration as a part of the *Catalog of Federal Domestic Assistance* (CFDA) and is presented here with appreciation expressed to that agency. It is specifically directed to the federal government's grant review and funding process, but many of the principles involved also can be applied in developing proposals to private foundations, state government agencies, and other organizations.

DEVELOPING A GRANT PROPOSAL

A successful grant proposal is one that is well prepared, thoughtfully planned, and concisely packaged. The potential applicant should become familiar with all of the pertinent program criteria related to the federal program for other funding sources from which assistance is sought. For federal proposals, refer to the information contact person listed in the CFDA program description before developing a proposal. Ask for information such as whether funding is available, when deadlines occur, and the process used by the grantor agency for accepting applications. Applicants should remember that the basic requirements, application forms, information, and procedures vary with the federal agency making the grant award.

Persons without prior grant proposal writing experience may find it useful to attend a grantsmanship workshop. Applicants interested in additional readings on grantsmanship and proposal development should consult the references listed here and explore other library resources.

Developing Ideas for the Proposal

When developing an idea for a proposal it is important to determine if the idea has been considered in the applicant's locality or state. A careful check should be made with legislators and area government agencies and related public and private agencies that may currently have grant awards or contracts to do similar work. If a similar program already exists, the applicant may need to reconsider submitting the proposed project, particularly if duplication of effort is perceived. If significant differences or improvements in the proposed project's goals can be clearly established, it may be worthwhile to pursue federal assistance.

Community Support

Community support for most proposals is essential. Once a proposal summary is developed, look for individuals or groups representing academic, political, professional, and lay organizations that may be willing to support the proposal in writing. The type and caliber of community support is critical in the initial and subsequent review phases. In some cases, letters of support can be persuasive to a grantor agency. Do not overlook support from local government agencies and public officials. Letters of endorsement detailing exact areas of project sanction and commitment are often requested as part of a proposal to a federal agency. Several months may be required to develop letters of endorsement since something of value (e.g., buildings, staff, services) is sometimes negotiated between the parties involved.

Many agencies require, in writing, affiliation agreements (a mutual agreement to share services between agencies) and building space commitments prior to either grant approval or award. A useful method of generating community support may be to hold meetings with the top decision makers in the community who would be concerned with the subject matter of the proposal. The forum for discussion may include a query into the merits of the proposal, development of a contract of support for the proposal, generating data in support of the proposal, or developing a strategy to create proposal support from a large number of community groups.

Identification of a Funding Resource

A review of the "Objectives and Uses" and "Use Restrictions" sections of the *Catalog of Federal Domestic Assistance* program description can point out which programs might provide funding for an idea. Do not overlook the related programs as potential resources. Both the applicant and the grantor agency should have the same interests, intentions, and needs if a proposal is to be considered an acceptable candidate for funding.

Once a potential grantor agency is identified, call the contact number given in "Information Contacts" and ask for a grant application kit. Later, get to know some of the grantor agency personnel. Ask for suggestions, criticisms, and advice about the proposed project. In many cases, the more agency personnel know about the proposal, the better the chance of support and of an eventual favorable decision. Sometimes it is useful to send the proposal summary to a specific agency official in a separate cover letter and ask for review and comment at the earliest possible convenience. Always check with the federal agency to determine its preference if this approach is under consideration. If the review is unfavorable and differences cannot be resolved, ask the examining agency (official) to suggest another department or agency that may be interested in the proposal. A personal visit to the agency's regional office or headquarters is also important. A visit not only establishes face-to-face contact, but it also may bring out some essential details about the proposal or help secure literature and references from the agency's library.

Federal agencies are required to report funding information as funds are approved, increased, or decreased among projects within a given state, depending on the type of required reporting. Also, consider reviewing the federal budget for the current and budget fiscal years to determine proposed dollar amounts for particular budget functions.

The applicant should carefully study the eligibility requirements for each federal program under consideration. The applicant may learn that he or she is required to provide services otherwise unintended, such as a service to particular client groups or involvement of specific institutions. It may necessitate the modification of the original concept in order for the project to be eligible for funding. Questions about eligibility should be discussed with the appropriate program officer.

Deadlines for submitting applications are often not negotiable. They are usually associated with strict timetables for agency review. Some programs have more than one application deadline during the fiscal year. Applicants should plan proposal development around the established deadlines.

Getting Organized to Write the Proposal

Throughout the proposal writing stage keep a notebook handy to write down ideas. Periodically, try to connect ideas by reviewing the notebook. Never throw away ideas you've jotted down during the grant writing stage. Maintain a file labeled "Ideas," or some other convenient title, and review it from time to time. The file should be easily accessible. The gathering of documents such as articles of incorporation, tax exemption certificates, and bylaws should be completed, if possible, before the writing begins.

REVIEW

At some point, perhaps after the first or second draft is completed, seek out a neutral third party to review the proposal working draft for continuity, clarity, and reasoning. Ask for constructive criticism at this point, rather than waiting for the federal grantor agency to volunteer this information during the review cycle. For example, has the writer made unsupported assumptions or used jargon or excessive language in the proposal?

Most proposals are made to institutions rather than individuals. Often signatures of chief administrative officials are required. Check to make sure they are included in the proposal wherever appropriate.

Proposals should be typed, collated, copied, and packaged correctly and neatly (according to agency instructions, if any). Each package should be inspected to ensure uniformity from cover to cover. Binding may require either clamps or hard covers. Check with the federal agency to determine its preference. A neat, organized, and attractive proposal package can leave a positive impression with the reader about the proposal contents.

A cover letter should always accompany a proposal. Standard U.S. Postal Service requirements apply unless otherwise indicated by the federal agency. Make sure there is enough time for the proposals to reach their destinations. Otherwise, special arrangements may be necessary. Always coordinate such arrangements with the federal grantor agency project office (the agency that will ultimately have the responsibility for the project), the grant office (the agency that will coordinate the grant review), and the contract office (the agency responsible for disbursement and grant award notices), if necessary.

WRITING THE GRANT PROPOSAL

There are eight basic components to creating a solid proposal package:

1. the proposal summary
2. introduction of organization
3. the problem statement (or needs assessment)
4. project objectives
5. project methods or design
6. project evaluation
7. future funding
8. the project budget

The following will provide an overview of these components.

The Proposal Summary: Outline of Project Goals

The proposal summary outlines the proposed project and should appear at the beginning of the proposal. It could be in the form of a cover letter or a separate page, but it should definitely be brief—no longer than two or three paragraphs. The summary would be most useful if it were prepared after the proposal has been developed in order to encompass all the key summary points necessary to communicate the objectives of the project. It is this document that becomes the cornerstone of your proposal, and the initial impression it gives will be critical to the success of your venture. In many cases, the summary will be the first part of the proposal package seen by agency officials and very possibly could be the only part of the package that is carefully reviewed before the decision is made to consider the project any further.

The applicant must select a fundable project that can be supported in view of the local need. Alternatives, in the absence of federal support, should be pointed out. The influence of the project, both during and after the project period, should be explained. The consequences of the project as a result of funding should be highlighted.

Introduction: Presenting a Credible Applicant or Organization

The applicant should gather data about its organization from all available sources. Most proposals require a description of an applicant's organization to describe its past and present operations. Some features to consider are:

- a brief biography of board members and key staff members
- the organization's goals, philosophy, track record with other grantors, and any success stories
- relevant data regarding the goals of the federal grantor agency that also establish the applicant's credibility

The Problem Statement: Stating the Purpose at Hand

The problem statement (or needs assessment) is a key element of a proposal that makes a clear, concise, and well-supported statement of the problem to be addressed. The best way to collect information about the problem is to conduct and document both a formal and informal needs assessment for a program in the target or service area. The information provided should be both factual and directly related to the problem addressed by the proposal.

Areas to document are:

1. The purpose for developing the proposal.
2. The beneficiaries—who are they and how will they benefit.
3. The social and economic costs to be affected.
4. The nature of the problem (provide as much hard evidence as possible).
5. How the applicant organization came to realize the problem exists, and what is currently being done about the problem.
6. The remaining alternatives available when funding has been exhausted. Explain what will happen to the project and the impending implications.
7. Most importantly, the specific manner through which problems might be solved.

Review the resources needed, considering how they will be used and to what end. There is a considerable body of literature on the exact assessment techniques to be used. Any local, regional, or state government planning office, or local university offering course work in planning and evaluation techniques should be able to provide excellent background references. Types of data that may be collected include: historical, geographic, quantitative, factual, statistical, and philosophical information, as well as studies completed by colleges and literature searches from public or university libraries. Local colleges or universities that have a department or section related to the proposal topic may help determine if there is interest in developing a student or faculty project to conduct a needs assessment. It may be helpful to include examples of the findings for highlighting in the proposal.

Project Objectives: Goals and Desired Outcome

Program objectives refer to specific activities in a proposal. It is necessary to identify all objectives related to the goals to be reached and the methods to be employed to achieve the stated objectives. Consider quantities or things measurable, and refer to a problem statement and the outcome of proposed activities when developing a well-stated objective. The figures used should be verifiable. Remember, if the proposal is funded, the stated objectives will probably be used to evaluate program progress, so be realistic. There is literature available to help identify and write program objectives.

Program Methods and Program Design: A Plan of Action

The program design refers to how the project is expected to work and solve the stated problem. Sketch out the following:

1. The activities to occur along with the related resources and staff needed to operate the project (inputs).
2. A flow chart of the organizational features of the project. Describe how the parts interrelate, where personnel will be needed, and what they are expected to do. Identify the kinds of facilities, transportation, and support services required (throughputs).

Explain what will be achieved through 1 and 2 above (outputs); i.e., plan for measurable results. Project staff may be required to produce evidence of program performance through an examination of stated objectives during either a site visit by the federal grantor agency and/or grant reviews that may involve peer review committees.

It may be useful to devise a diagram of the program design. For example, draw a three column block. Each column is headed by one of the parts (inputs, throughputs, and outputs), and on the left (next to the first column) specific program features should be identified (i.e., implementation, staffing, procurement, and systems development). In the grid, specify something about the program design. For example, assume the first column is labeled "inputs" and the first row is labeled "staff." On the grid one might specify under inputs "five nurses to operate a child care unit." The throughput might be to "maintain charts, counsel the children, and set up a daily routine;" outputs might be to "discharge 25 healthy children per week." This type of procedure will help to conceptualize both the scope and detail of the project.

Wherever possible, justify in the narrative the course of action taken. The most economical method should be used that does not compromise or sacrifice project quality. The financial expenses associated with performance of the project will later become points of negotiation with the federal program staff. If everything is not carefully justified in writing in the proposal, after negotiation with the federal grantor agencies, the approved project may resemble less of the original concept. Carefully consider the pressures of the proposed implementation, that is, the time and money needed to acquire each part of the plan. A Program Evaluation and Review Technique (PERT) chart could be useful and supportive in justifying some proposals.

Highlight the innovative features of the proposal, which could be considered distinct from other proposals under consideration.

Whenever possible, use appendices to provide details, supplementary data, references, and information requiring in-depth analysis. These types of data, although supportive of the proposal, if included in the body of the design, could detract from its readability. Appendices provide the proposal reader with immediate access to details if and when clarification of an idea, sequence, or conclusion is required. Timetables, work plans, schedules, activities, methodologies, legal papers, personal vitae, letters of support, and endorsements are examples of appendices.

Evaluation: Product and Process Analysis

The evaluation component is twofold: product evaluation and process evaluation. Product evaluation addresses results that can be attributed to the project, as well as the extent to which the project has satisfied its desired objectives. Process evaluation addresses how the project was conducted, in terms of consistency with the stated plan of action and the effectiveness of the various activities within the plan.

Most federal agencies now require some form of program evaluation among grantees. The requirements of the proposed project should be explored carefully. Evaluations may be conducted by an internal staff member, an evaluation firm, or both. The applicant should state the amount of time needed to evaluate, how the feedback will be distributed among the proposed staff, and a schedule for review and comment for this type of communication. Evaluation designs may start at the beginning, middle, or end of a project, but the applicant should specify a start-up time. It is practical to submit an evaluation design at the start of a project for two reasons: convincing evaluations require the collection of appropriate data before and during program operations, and, if the evaluation design cannot be prepared at the outset, then a critical review of the program design may be advisable.

Even if the evaluation design has to be revised as the project progresses, it is much easier and cheaper to modify a good design. If the problem is not well defined and carefully analyzed for cause and effect relationships, then a good evaluation design may be difficult to achieve. Sometimes a pilot study is needed to begin the identification of facts and relationships. Often, a thorough literature search may be sufficient.

Evaluation requires both coordination and agreement among program decision makers (if known). Above all, the federal grantor agency's requirements should be highlighted in the evaluation design. Also, federal grantor agencies may require specific evaluation techniques, such as designated data formats (an existing information collection system), or they may offer financial inducements for voluntary participation in a national evaluation study. The applicant should ask specifically about these points. Also, consult the "Criteria for Selecting Proposals" section of the *Catalog* program description to determine the exact evaluation methods to be required for the program if funded.

Future Funding: Long-Term Project Planning

Describe a plan for continuation beyond the grant period and/or the availability of other resources necessary to implement the grant. Discuss maintenance and future program funding if the program is for construction activity. Account for other needed expenditures if the program includes purchase of equipment.

The Proposal Budget: Planning the Budget

Funding levels in federal assistance programs change yearly. It is useful to review the appropriations over the past several years to try to project future funding levels (see the "Financial Information" section of the *Catalog* program description). However, it is safer to never anticipate that the income from the grant will be the sole support for the project. This consideration should be given to the overall budget requirements and, in particular, to budget line items most subject to inflationary pressures. Restraint is important in determining inflationary cost projections (avoid padding budget line items), but attempt to anticipate possible future increases.

Some vulnerable budget areas are: utilities, rental of buildings and equipment, salary increases, food, telephones, insurance, and transportation. Budget adjustments are sometimes made after the grant award, but this can be a lengthy process. Be certain that implementation, continuation, and phase-down costs can be met. Consider costs associated with leases, evaluation systems, hard/ soft match requirements, audits, development, implementation and maintenance of information and accounting systems, and other long-term financial commitments.

A well-prepared budget justifies all expenses and is in line with the proposal narrative. Some parts of the budget will need to be evaluated for consistency. For example:

1. The salaries in the proposal in relation to those of the applicant organization should be similar.
2. If new staff persons are being hired, additional space and equipment should be considered, as necessary.
3. If the budget calls for an equipment purchase, it should be the type allowed by the grantor agency.
4. If additional space is rented, the increase in insurance should be supported.
5. If an indirect cost rate applies to the proposal, the division between direct and indirect costs should not be in conflict, and the aggregate budget totals should refer directly to the approved formula.
6. If matching costs are required, the contributions to the matching fund should be taken out of the budget, unless otherwise specified in the application instructions.

It is very important to become familiar with governmentwide circular requirements. The *Catalog of Federal Domestic Assistance* identifies in the program description section (as information is provided from the agencies) the particular circulars applicable to a federal program and summarizes coordination of Executive Order 12372 "Intergovernmental Review of Programs" requirements in its appendix. The applicant should thoroughly review the appropriate circulars since they are essential in determining items such as cost principles and in conforming with government guidelines for federal domestic assistance.

GLOSSARY

SELECTED TERMS RELATED TO FUND-RAISING

Advancement.   The efforts to represent an organization to the public or generate external support, or the organizational area devoted to such efforts.

Award.   Financial assistance, or related forms of assistance, usually designated for a specific purpose.

Award letter.   An official notification of a grant or contract award.

Beneficiary.   The recipient of funds for a trust or insurance policy.

Bequest.   A gift designated through a will.

Bricks and mortar.   A slang term for building projects or projects where funds for construction are raised.

CASE.   The Council for Advancement and Support of Education.

Case statement.   A written statement spelling out an organization's need for support.

CFDA.   The *Catalog of Federal Domestic Assistance.*

CFRE.   Certified Fund Raising Executive, a professional designation awarded by the National Society of Fund Raising Executives.

Charitable gift annuity.   An arrangement between an individual and a nonprofit organization in which the donor receives a fixed income based on earnings from a donation made to the organization.

146

Charitable lead trust. An arrangement through which the interest from an annuity or unitrust is given annually to a qualifying organization.

Charitable remainder annuity trust. An arrangement in which a donor gives property while receiving a specific percentage of its value for the remainder of the donor's lifetime.

Contract. An agreement between a government agency and a recipient in which specific services are to be performed or actions are to be taken in return for monetary payment.

CRD. The Council for Resource Development (formerly the National Council for Resource Development).

Development. Roughly synonymous with advancement, the functional area of an organization dedicated to seeking external support, or the practice of seeking such support.

Direct mail fund-raising. Solicitation of gifts by letter or other mailed information.

Endowed funds. Funds that are invested with the intent of earning interest income without spending the principle.

Grant. An award of financial assistance, usually of money but sometimes of equipment or other property, made by an organization to a grantee.

Grantee. The recipient of a grant.

In-kind contributions. Contributions made for a grantee toward a project; similar to matching funds but in noncash contributions.

Matching funds. Funds contributed by a grantee or third party toward a grant budget.

Nonprofit. Established for noncommercial purposes, usually with a role of serving the public or some component of the public in a charitable, educational, or other worthwhile way.

NSFRE. The National Society of Fund Raising Executives.

Planned giving. The practice of planning deferred gifts, usually as a part of estate planning, with the gifts to go to eligible nonprofit organizations.

Pre-application.   A preliminary proposal submitted in advance of a full proposal.

Prospect.   A potential donor, often identified by the level of gift a prospective donor is capable of making.

Prospect research.   Background research to obtain information about a donor or potential donors.

RFP.   A Request for Proposal, or invitation to submit a grant application or other proposal.

Subgrant.   An award made by a grantee to another organization or other eligible party.

Stewardship.   The ongoing recognition of donors and friends of an organization.

Trust.   A formal arrangement conveying money or other property where it is held by a trustee on behalf of a specified person, persons, or organization.

Unsolicited proposal.   A grant proposal or other application submitted without an RFP having been issued.